KIM & KANYE

The Love Story

KIM & KANYE

The Love Story

NADIA COHEN

JOHN BLAKE

Published by John Blake Publishing Ltd,
3 Bramber Court, 2 Bramber Road,
London W14 9PB, England

www.johnblakepublishing.co.uk

www.facebook.com/johnblakebooks ▊

twitter.com/jblakebooks ▊

This edition published in 2014

ISBN: 978 1 78418 029 4

British Library Cataloguing-in-Publication Data:

A catalogue record for this book is available from the British Library.

Design by www.envydesign.co.uk

Printed in Great Britain by CPI Group (UK) Ltd

1 3 5 7 9 10 8 6 4 2

Papers used by John Blake Publishing are natural, recyclable products made
from wood grown in sustainable forests. The manufacturing processes
conform to the environmental regulations of the country of origin.

Every attempt has been made to contact the relevant copyright-holders,
but some were unobtainable. We would be grateful if the
appropriate people could contact us.

For Harry, Felix and Dan -
the best boys I know.

CONTENTS

CHAPTER 1

HUMBLE – AND NOT SO HUMBLE – BEGINNINGS

Although Kim Kardashian and Kanye West appear to be a match made in heaven, the Hollywood power couple began their lives worlds apart.

Kimberly Noel Kardashian was born on 21 October 1980 into a life of unimaginable luxury. Alongside her sisters Kourtney, Khloe, Kendall, Kylie, and brother Rob, Kim's indulgent upbringing was like something out of a fairy tale. Her father was the multi-millionaire lawyer Robert Kardashian, who gained notoriety when he defended his best friend, OJ Simpson, at his controversial murder trial. He had met Kim's mother, Kristen Mary Houghton, in 1972, at a racetrack in San Diego, having been introduced by a mutual friend. She was just seventeen at the time, and working as a flight attendant, while Robert was a law student eleven years her senior. Despite the age gap, the pair were smitten and married within four years, deciding to raise their family in a sprawling mansion on Tower Lane, one of the most exclusive addresses in star-studded Beverly Hills.

There were only three houses in the exclusive cul-de-sac. One belonged to the world-famous singer Bruce Springsteen, and on the other side lived an eccentric millionaire who kept a garden full of peacocks and llamas. Chat show host Jay Leno was a close neighbour too. The Kardashian kids had everything they could wish for – dozens of pets including cats named Coco and Chanel, hamsters, turtles, Doberman and Bichon Frisé dogs, even a woodpecker and four white mice named Eenie, Meanie, Miney and Moe.

Tucked away at the end of that private road, behind a long drive, their vast home boasted a pool shaped like a duck alongside an egg-shaped jacuzzi. There was a tennis court, and a pool house with a bar. Little wonder then that the Kardashian compound was where all the local children wanted to hang out. In her book, *Kardashian Konfidential*, Kim recalled how her friends used to come over for tennis lessons, and Kris brought out Girl Scout cookies and ice tea to wash them down with. She said that those times would forever be embedded in the minds of her and her sisters.

The children had an idyllic childhood, full of fun and over-the-top birthday parties with pony rides and petting zoos. Kim even celebrated her fourteenth birthday at Michael Jackson's famous ranch, Neverland, where she and her friends enjoyed amusement park rides, movies and a zoo with baby elephants!

The parties their parents threw were legendary too, and

gave Kim a flair for lavish entertaining which would be evident when she married Kanye many years later. She recalled one New Year's Eve celebration with a can-can theme when Kris sent out life-size chocolate legs as invitations: 'Our parents just loved to entertain and have people over – and people just loved coming over to be entertained! Tower Lane was truly party central.'

Giving an insight into their close-knit family bond, which was to characterise them later in life, Kim explained in her book *Kardashian Konfidential* that Christmas had always been a favourite holiday of hers. Her mum Kris used to decorate the entire house from top to bottom after Thanksgiving, complete with a themed tree which changed each year. Every Christmas Eve would see a huge party descend on the Kardashian household, and sometimes her father would dress up as Santa (Kim added that she had believed in Santa for far longer than most of her friends!).

She remembered how the family would wake up at five or six in the morning, and the house would be charged with nervous energy and excitement.

But sometimes sibling rivalry would spoil the festive harmony: one year Kim ended up in tears because she received a fish tank instead of what she'd asked for, but her siblings would usually get the things on their lists. One year, Kim had asked for a watch she had wanted all year, and didn't get it – and then it turned out that Kourtney, who was one year ahead of her in school, got the very same watch for her graduation present.

After her parents divorced in 1991, the girls would usually go to Robert's house for the afternoons and later eat dinner with Khloe's godparent, the boxer Sugar Ray Leonard, and his wife at their house.

Kim said that her most memorable Christmas was the year when her dad walked in unannounced and threw a set of keys at Khloe. It turned out he had given her a brand new Mercedes! The whole family were excited by that gift.

For Robert, family was more important than anything else. Despite his high-flying career, he was fully involved in his children's daily routines, would check their homework and even coached school soccer games. He insisted they always had dinner together, banned phones from the table and every night would go around asking everyone to say what was 'the peak and the pit' of their day. Although he has long since passed away, the family still play 'The Peak and The Pit' when they gather together for special occasions.

When asked recently about the peaks and pits of her life, Kim said in her book *Kardashian Konfidential* that the biggest peak was her great, happy childhood, and making her greatest friends, people she'd known since pre-school and who she knew would stay with her for life.

As for the pits, she highlighted her 'annoying' relationship history, claiming she felt one hundred years old and bored of the dating game.

Needless to say, Kardashian family holidays were equally lavish affairs – to Mexico, Palm Springs or Hawaii, and Thanksgiving was always spent skiing in the exclusive Colorado mountain resort of Vail, where they would rent a luxurious house with a hot tub and indoor swimming pool.

Meanwhile, Kanye West had a vastly different upbringing

from his future wife. Born on 8 June 1977 in Atlanta, Georgia, by the time he was three his parents had divorced and he moved with his mother Donda to Chicago. His political activist father Ray was a member of the Black Panther Party, a revolutionary socialist organisation active in the United States from 1966 until 1982. The party gained international notoriety with its doctrine calling for the protection of black neighbourhoods from police brutality.

Ray was also one of the first black photojournalists at The Atlanta Journal-Constitution, and later became a Christian counsellor. In 2006, Kanye helped him open The Good Water Store and Café in Maryland. The rapper's mother, Dr. Donda C. Williams West, was a Professor of English at Clark Atlanta University, and became the Chair of the English Department at Chicago State University before retiring to become Kanye's manager.

When Kanye was ten, he and Donda moved to Nanjing, China, where she was teaching as part of a university exchange programme. According to his mother, Kanye was the only foreigner in his class, but settled in well and quickly picked up the language, although he has since forgotten most of it. When asked about his grades in high school, West replied with a typical lack of modesty: 'I got A's and B's. And I'm not even frontin'.

Kanye showed a talent for the arts from an early age; he began writing poetry and became passionate about music when he was just five years old. As a teenager growing up back in Chicago, he became deeply involved in the city's hip-hop scene, and started writing musical raps, which he sold to other artists. At the age of thirteen, Kanye wrote his first rap song, called 'Green Eggs and Ham', and managed to persuade Donda to pay $25 an hour for him to have recording sessions in a small basement recording studio, where a microphone hung from the ceiling by a wire clothes hanger. His first recording had been inspired by his favourite childhood book by Dr Seuss, and showed an early talent for rapping.

Although this was far from the career that highly academic Donda had imagined for her son, she supported him and paid for the studio time he wanted. At fifteen, while still a student at West Aurora High School, Kanye met and formed a close friendship with a producer called No I.D., also known as 'The Godfather of Chicago Hip Hop'. No I.D. soon became his mentor, and taught Kanye how to sample and programme beats. In 1997 Kanye won a scholarship to attend Chicago's American Academy of Art and began taking painting classes, but shortly after transferred to Chicago State University to major in English, much to his mother's relief.

However, it soon became apparent to Kanye that his busy class schedule was interfering with his music, and at the age of twenty he made the decision to drop out of college to pursue his dream of becoming a musician. His mother, who was a professor at the university, was devastated when her son abandoned his studies. In an interview with Chicago Tribune, she said 'It was drummed into my head that college is the ticket to a good life, but some career goals don't require college.' She said later: 'For Kanye to make an album called *College Dropout* it was more about having the guts to embrace who you are, rather than following the path society has carved out for you.'

While Kanye was ambitious and working hard to follow his chosen career in the highly competitive music world in his twenties, Kim's life was a whirlwind of parties and shopping as she became known as one of Hollywood's best connected socialites. She was hanging out with a high-profile group of 'It Girls', including Paris Hilton, and openly admitted that her ambition in life was to be a reality TV star.

Busy trying to find a way to move into the spotlight, Kim took it coolly in her stride when her parents divorced in 1991, and her mother married Olympic athlete Bruce Jenner, just five months after meeting him on a blind date. In *Kardashian Konfidential*, she said perhaps she was less affected by the divorce because she was so anxious over the overwhelming changes to her body. The splitting up of her parents happened to coincide with the hormone-fuelled upheaval of puberty, and Kim was becoming upset with how she was developing physically. Whilst she had always had a 'big butt', it was her breasts which were bothering her. She was so embarrassed and struggling to cope with the scary side of transforming into an adult.

She recalled sitting in the bathtub and putting hot cloths over her breasts to try and shrink them back down, whilst praying that they had done growing. Her mother Kris had always said she would one day embrace those curves – and she was right. Kim owns her curvaceous body like no one else these days.

Kim had started to become body conscious from an early age. By the age of eleven she was having her eyebrows waxed by her mother, and by thirteen she was getting bikini waxes.

After Kris and Robert's divorce, the girls attended an all-girls Catholic school and divided their time between two homes – they would spend ten days with their mother, followed by five days with their father. She later asserted that both her parents always made sure they put their girls first. Even in the midst of their divorce, they united and never tried to win favour at the other's expense. It opened Kim's eyes to a whole new way to relate to her family.

But their lives were thrown into chaos in 1994 when basketball player OJ Simpson was arrested for the murder of his wife, Nicole. Fiercely loyal, Robert renewed his legal licence and vowed to defend OJ, who even stayed at their house in the aftermath of his wife's shocking death. Robert passionately believed in his innocence. Suddenly thrust into the glare of the public eye, the family received death threats, and were publicly abused, but Kim said later that they never answered when people asked what their thoughts on the trial outcome were. It was such a painful and traumatic period for all the family that it continues to shape who they are today, and is not up for discussion.

Despite his wealth, Robert was determined not to spoil his children. Although he brought each of them cars in high school he made them sign legal-style contracts promising to keep their grades up and when Kim had a crash in her BMW when she was sixteen, he made her work in a clothing store to pay for the repairs. In *Kardashian Konfidential*, she recalled that she didn't appreciate her parents' efforts to teach them responsibility at the time, but now she is incredibly grateful for the iron work ethic it taught her.

Robert also taught his children that money would not buy them happiness, and took them all to see homeless people to help them understand how blessed they were.

Kim remained close to her father until his death, aged fifty-nine, from oesophageal cancer in 2003, just eight weeks after he was diagnosed with the disease. Six weeks before his death he remarried and most of his fortune went to his new wife. Kim spoke movingly at his funeral and has since said that after Robert's death, the family forged an even tighter bond than before, saying 'We exchange "I love you's" more since our dad died. He used to say it all the time to us. He'd never get off the phone without an "I love you" and we all still do that with each other.'

CHAPTER 2

GROWING UP

Had they met in their teens, Kim and Kanye would probably have loathed each other. While he was hanging out with the bad boys of rap in the Chicago underworld, Kim was a squeaky-clean Madonna fan and dated Michael Jackson's nephew TJ for five years.

But when that relationship broke up, Kim found it hard to bounce back and started to feel insecure about her shapely body, admitting that she often didn't feel skinny enough. Being a super-curvy girl, she got used to not seeing any models or high-profile celebrities with a figure like hers.

'This really great relationship I had in high school ended. I thought everything had been perfect and I didn't understand why we were breaking up, and it was really hard on me.

'From that moment on I began to feel a loss of self-esteem. And I gained a little bit of weight, maybe from trying to use food to comfort myself, and the extra weight made me feel worse.

'After that I would date anyone who would give me attention. People that I knew on some level just weren't good for me. I knew I was unhappy, but I couldn't bring myself to say so. I might try to end the relationship but then I would hold back because I had such a difficult time coming out and saying something that might hurt someone else. It wasn't just guys. I let people treat me any way they wanted and never stood up for myself. I was a doormat.

'I was very dependent on people so I would go from boyfriend to boyfriend and never had a chance to be single.'

When she was nineteen Kim shocked her family by marrying Damon Thomas, a music producer ten years her senior, in a whirlwind Vegas wedding which she attempted to keep secret from her sisters. But after Kourtney found her marriage certificate online, she told their parents, who were furious. Kim was so angry she refused to speak to her sister for four months: 'That was definitely the longest time any of us ever were in a fight,' Kim revealed. 'Nothing since has come close.'

The marriage lasted three years, and they ended on bad terms.

But Kim's father forgave her and gave his daughter her first job at his company Movie Tunes, which supplies music to cinemas. Kim spent her days burning and sending out CDs, and there was no special treatment for the boss's daughter, and she admitted that it was a good lesson for later in life, and taught her the valuable lesson that she could be business-like with people that she was close with.

A self-confessed shopaholic, Kim quickly moved on and set up her own business organising the contents of people's wardrobes, and later became a stylist to celebrity clients, including her friend Paris Hilton. In *Kardashian Konfidential* she recalled how she stumbled upon the idea of becoming a professional stylist. As a stylist, she learned some good tricks for highlighting her best features – accentuating her sister Khloe's long legs was one example, but her mother Kris had never liked her arms and Kim always managed to hide them when planning an outfit for her. For herself, the most important thing was to try to accentuate her curvy figure and narrow waist by using belts to play with perspective.

She also learned to stay on top of the latest fashion trends by shopping around in as many different outlets as possible – and not just the high-end stores. Some of Kim's favourites include Zara, Forever 21 and H&M, and some of her unique styles come from mixing and matching between them all. Because the best trends always sell out so quickly, and often the stores only stock a few of each item, she always makes a point of coming back to keep tabs on the latest arrivals – a trick which has paid dividends for her wherever she's gone.

Kim's style has kept on changing in recent years – her preference in the early days was for a totally casual daytime look which favoured comfortable outfits and flip-flops or soft shoes, before switching up entirely in the evenings by dressing to the nines. Tight, short dresses with huge teased-out hair and devastatingly fancy shoes were the order of the night. But in recent times, Kim has toned down her evening outfits, trying to offset great clothes with more edgy looks, like wearing vests over her dresses. The most crucial thing for her is to make sure that her style is changing day-to-day and never getting stale. She's even renounced wearing sweatpants, preferring to go with a jeans or leggings look. In her words, 'I spend a lot of time lugging things through airports so why not look cute doing it?'

Just as her business was starting to evolve, Kim decided to take control of her personal life too, and the year after her father died, she divorced Damon. In *Kardashian Konfidential* she explained that losing your love can help see other things more clearly in life. Whilst she may not have known what she wanted, she knew what she didn't want and that it was time to move forwards.

Kim left Beverly Hills and travelled the world with friends, vowing to take a year off men as well as work. While opening her eyes to new cultures, she also found that her shapely figure could work to her advantage: 'I started to get attention for my curves,' she recalled. 'Exactly the thing I'd been trying to get rid of for so long!

'I used to think maybe I didn't attract the right kind of people because I didn't look the way they wanted me to. I hadn't figured out yet that the real reason I wasn't attracting the right kind of person was because I am such a people pleaser. I wasn't putting out my own sense of self-worth.'

She added that she would no longer take the way she had been treated in the past and was much more assertive now.

Kim started to get used to finding herself making headlines when she dated the American pop singer Nick Lachey, shortly after he had very publicly split from actress Jessica Simpson.

The paparazzi followed them to the cinema, and the next night she was spotted at a nightclub with Paris Hilton, who taught her how to deal with the barrage of flashbulbs: Paris told her to always make sure she was smiling – and at all costs to avoid saying anything under your breath because of the press's recent tendency to carry video cameras at all times to catch unwitting celebrities out.

Around the same time, thousands of miles away on the other side of the country, Kanye West was enjoying his first taste of fame too, as he started producing records for more established artists. He produced eight tracks for a Chicago rapper named Grav, and also music for Deric D-Dot Angelettie. Unable to release a solo album, Kanye formed a group called the Go Getters, who released their first and only album, *World Record Holders*, in 1999. Meanwhile he produced a track for Foxy Brown's album, *Chyna Doll*, which became the first hip-hop album by a female rapper to debut at the top of the US Billboard chart in its first week of release.

Kanye got his big break in 2000 when he began to produce for artists on Roc-A-Fella Records in LA, and he is often credited with revitalising Jay-Z's career with his contributions to the rapper's influential 2001 album, *The Blueprint*. He also worked on hits for Ludacris, Alicia Keys and Janet Jackson.

He still wanted to be a rapper, although many labels ignored him because he did not portray the 'gangsta' image that was popular in mainstream hip-hop at the time. Eventually the label's boss Damon Dash signed him to Roc-A-Fella Records to keep him from defecting to a rival label.

Kanye had a breakthrough when, in October 2002, he fell

asleep at the wheel of his car after working late. The crash left him with a shattered jaw, which had to be wired shut, and the accident inspired him to write the song 'Through the Wire' while he was recovering. That song laid the foundation for his mix tape, *Get Well Soon*, which was released in December 2002: 'All the better artists have expressed what they were going through,' he said later. 'The album was my medicine.'

He immediately started work on his debut album, *The College Dropout*, and when asked to explain his theme Kanye said: 'Make your own decisions. Don't let society tell you, "This is what you have to do."'

After purchasing his first of what would be many, many designer items, Kanye carried all his ideas in a Louis Vuitton backpack filled with old discs and demo tapes. Once complete, the album was leaked months before its release but Kanye decided to remaster and revise certain tracks. He took the opportunity to meticulously refine the production, adding string arrangements, gospel choirs and new verses. His perfectionist streak meant the release was postponed three times before it was eventually released in February 2004, shooting to number two on the Billboard chart, while his single, 'Through the Wire', peaked at number fifteen. His second single, 'Slow Jamz', featuring the actor Jamie Foxx, was his first number one. The album received universal acclaim and has consistently been ranked among the great hip-hop works. It was eventually certified triple platinum, winning ten Grammy nominations. Kanye West had arrived.

CHAPTER 3

LOVE AT
FIRST SIGHT?

Kim was fast becoming something of a global superstar, and after posing fully nude in *Playboy* in 2007 her celebrity status was confirmed. She later told how she regretted the raunchy shoot, and blamed her mother for pushing her into it: in an interview with Harper's Bazaar Kim said: 'I was uncomfortable. My mom told me to go for it: "They might never ask you again. Our show isn't on the air yet. No one knows who you are. Do it and you'll have these beautiful pictures to look at when you're my age."'

She was hanging out in the most exclusive circles but was still ambitious and since her father had instilled all his children with a strong work ethic, she was determined to earn her own money.

But that famous *Playboy* shoot, and another photo of her showing off her toned legs next to then best friend Paris Hilton during a visit to Australia some months earlier, had caught Kanye's attention, although he did not make a move.

In September 2007, however, the planets aligned and the couple met for the first time at a party thrown by Intermix in Beverly Hills. Cupid's arrow had struck, but the timing was not ideal as Kanye was seeing designer Alexis Phifer, who he started dating in 2002 and became engaged to in 2006. Kim was also off the market, as she had just started seeing New Orleans Saints football player Reggie Bush. After Kanye split from Alexis in 2008, he hooked up with model Amber Rose, while Kim's romance with Reggie went from strength to strength.

But Kim and Kanye ran into each other once again at a fashion show for the designer Y-3 at New York Fashion Week in February 2009. Kim was photographed hanging on to Reggie as she sat next to actress Milla Jovovich, while an uncomfortable-looking Kanye looked on as his crush just intensified.

In October 2010 Kim moved to New York to expand her business empire with a new clothing store, and among the first famous names to walk through the doors of her store Dash was none other than Mr Kanye West. As he strutted in, and warmly embraced the hostess, onlookers noticed the immediate chemistry.

Kim claimed she had invited him to the store in the city's trendy SoHo district for some style advice but the rapper was openly flirting with her as he looked over plans for the shop. Looking cool in a pair of aviator sunglasses and a black suit, Kanye admitted he was a bit surprised at the news that the sisters intended to open their store just two weeks later but he did accept Kim's flirty invitation to her thirtieth birthday party in Las Vegas a few days later.

It was clear that Kanye and Kim were very comfortable with each other as they chatted while Kourtney and her boyfriend, reality TV star Scott Disick, looked on. It had been revealed that Kim was hoping to find a man during her three-month stay in Manhattan, and it looked as if she had her sights firmly set on Kanye. An article in the *New York Post* newspaper explained the sisters' plan: 'They'll be using a penthouse at the Smyth Hotel for three months while they expand the family business and find Kim a man.

'A source said Scott Disick and baby Mason will live in the penthouse with Kourtney for the shoot, with the intention of relocating the family to New York permanently.'

By this stage Kim's empire already boasted several fashion boutiques, including another branch of their clothing shop Dash in Miami, but the girls had their sights set on New York, although they eventually decided not to relocate there permanently.

During their visit, Kim and Kourtney took the city by storm as they expanded their lucrative portfolio of assets, which already included a clothing line, a production company, fragrance and endorsements, which were amassing them millions of dollars. They were also filming their spin-off show, *Kim and Kourtney Take New York*, but still found plenty of time to party.

As well as her glitzy bash in Las Vegas, Kanye was also invited to celebrate Kim's birthday with the family a couple of days after visiting the new shop. He was among a very select group of friends invited to her private party on a luxury yacht in New York harbour, where they enjoyed a wedding-style triple-tiered white cake and cupcakes.

The VIP bash disappointed fans, who had expected to see Kim at a nightclub, but she explained via Twitter: 'I've already had my birthday club celebrations at Tao in Vegas and NYC and there are NO other birthday parties this weekend. Tonight I'll be having a private celebration with my friends and family, and then the birthday celebrations will be over.'

Although Kim and Kanye certainly had fun during that initial trip to New York, they decided to keep their budding romance casual as Kim wanted to play the field a little longer following her split earlier in the year from Reggie. And so she dated another American football star Miles Austin, Jennifer Lopez's former husband Cris Judd, Halle Berry's ex Gabriel Aubry, and just two months after first meeting Kanye she was linked to New York Nets basketball star Kris Humphries, who would later become her second husband.

Rumours started to fly when she and Kris were spotted partying up a storm at the Z100's Jingle Ball concert at Madison Square Garden in December 2010. Wearing a distinctive long white fur coat and gold heels, Kim was later spotted sneaking her latest flame into the Provocateur lounge, where they partied until 2am.

The couple then left together and headed back to the Smyth Hotel, just a day after Kim had been spotted courtside at the Nets game against the Los Angeles Lakers.

But just as Kim seemed to be having the time of her life – it had emerged that she raked in a staggering $6m that year – she came under fire for gaining 10lb in weight, with commentators remarking that she looked pregnant.

She told US celebrity chef Rachael Ray on her daytime chat show that she had fallen off the workout wagon because she had been having so much fun as she filmed *Kim and Kourtney Take New York*.

'I pride myself on working out and being very good,' she said. 'But when I went to New York, I went to Europe for three weeks before that and then here for six weeks, I went to the gym just one time – I'm humiliated to say that.

'I gained like 10 pounds and of course all over the internet it's like, "I'm pregnant". But I got it together.'

Kim also admitted that, despite all the dating she had been doing in recent months, she was determined to stay single: 'I'm definitely dating and I'm having a good time,' she said. 'But I made a promise to myself and I'm really trying to stick to it, but I'm such a hopeless romantic, it's hard. I want to try to be single my whole year of being thirty.

'I don't think it will last – that's just how I am. But the fact that I am trying is a really big step for me.'

Despite her public protests, Kim was clearly looking for romance, and just days later she was filmed on a date with actor Michael Copon. They were spotted kissing on her hotel balcony following a lunchtime date, and the scenes were shown in the season premiere of *Kourtney and Kim Take New York* on American entertainment channel *E!*

Kim and Copon had known each other since appearing together in the 2009 TV series *Beyond the Break*, but when he failed to ask her out, she was not impressed. 'I don't chase people. I've just been dropping hints that I'm single,' she told Kourtney on the show. 'I can't believe I've had the balls to call Michael and ask him out.'

She later insisted that she had taken time out from men, claiming, 'I gained so much confidence and broadened my horizons. And I had a blast. It was absolutely essential.'

But that romance burnt out quickly too, and just six months after she had first met 6ft 9in basketball star Kris Humphries, they surprised the world by announcing their engagement.

He proposed with a giant 20.5-carat ring and, of course, TV cameras were there to capture the whole romantic scene. Naturally, their lavish wedding ceremony, for which Kim wore a £15,000 Vera Wang dress, was screened on TV and the photos were sold to *People Magazine* for £1million in the late summer of 2011.

At the time she could not contain her excitement at having met the man of her dreams. Kim gushed in *Kardashian Konfidential* that she believed the best way to attract men is to be your own woman, and interesting in your own right. In her opinion, a woman should want someone who is ambitious and focused on pursuing goals and opportunities of their own. Kim believes that the more care and attention a man shows to his own life the more he is likely to show to yours; she also confesses she finds a strong sense of confidence and enthusiasm attractive.

She also alluded to her husband Kris and the admiration she has for his determination and attitude to life. She recalled how the fact that they were both so busy with their life and work was a mutual factor of attraction. She added that whilst each of us are responsible for creating satisfaction in our lives, the act of pursuing your goals and dreams might lead to you being the goal of someone else, and then who knows what could happen?

Preparing for her wedding had brought up lots of feelings. She found herself thinking about how happy and proud her father would have been to see her big day. Kim even dug out an old Tommy Bahama shirt he always used to wear and from the material she cut a small heart which she then sewed into the gown over her own heart.

Their happiness was not to last, however, and they announced that the marriage was over after just 72 days. By Halloween their relationship was over, with Kim citing 'irreconcilable differences' and filing for divorce.

It was not long before Kanye swooped in, and some cruel cynics (including her estranged husband) suggested that the entire relationship with Kris had been nothing more than a publicity stunt dreamed up by Kim to boost her profile and TV ratings. However, in an episode of *Keeping Up With The Kardashians*, a broken-hearted Kim sobbed as she explained how upset she was by the split.

Ironically, shortly after she filed for divorce, Kim appeared in a film called *The Marriage Counsellor*, although she did not play the wife. The film documents the experience of a woman named Judith, who cheats on her husband despite being a relationship expert. Kim took on the role of Judith's co-worker Ava, who uses her makeover skills to give her friend a confidence boost in the wake of her relationship crisis.

'She's trying to focus on the film and do her job and then get back home and lay low,' a source told *People Magazine*. But within days of the split being made public, rumours of a fresh love interest were in the air.

According to a report in the *New York Daily News*, Kanye was 'all over Kim' at an after-party following his 'Watch The Throne' concert in Los Angeles in December 2011, and it was becoming increasingly difficult for the pair to deny their blossoming romance. 'Kanye was eating Kim up like she was a piece of cake,' a source told the newspaper. 'He was all over her – caressing her head, touching her waist. I think he was dying to kiss her, but there were too many people in the room.'

The pair were attending billionaire Ron Burkle's party for Kanye and his friend, the rapper Jay-Z, who performed tracks from their hit album *Watch the Throne* at LA's Staples Center.

Kim's mother Kris, as well as sisters Khloe and Kourtney, were also in the VIP section, as at one point in the concert Kanye leaned over the stage to greet them all. Kim spent the evening dancing and swigging champagne from a bottle. The next day she tweeted: 'Last night was KRAY', referring to a lyric on one of Kanye's album tracks.

By January 2012 the worst-kept secret in show business was out. They had always insisted they were just friends who happened to have known each other for years but claims that there was nothing between Kim and Kanye were called into question just weeks after the concert when Kanye's ex, model Amber Rose, suggested that his closeness to Kim had led to their split.

Although gossip was beginning to appear about whether Kim and Kanye might be falling for each other, they both continued to date other people. In February Kanye was rumoured to be dating Victoria's Secret model Kate Upton, while Kim was forced to deny speculation that she was seeing American footballer Mark Sanchez after website *Strawberryicecream.com* reported that they were indulging in secret meetings in New York.

The website claimed a source said: 'Kim and Mark like to meet in hotels for dinner dates. Whenever Kim is in New York, they hang out.'

But Kim wrote on Twitter that she did not even know the sportsman, who had also dated *Heroes* star Hayden Panettiere: 'Dating rumours are always fun when u don't even know the people you're supposedly linked to! Who makes this stuff up!'

But by April there were no more denials. Kim and Kanye appeared to have given up on trying to hide their relationship, and were inseparable during a trip to New York. Kim, who has been known to change her outfits several times a day, was seen wearing the same pair of leather trousers for twenty-four hours, and they were spotted going into her hotel together after she flew in from Los Angeles. The next day she was seen sneaking out of Kanye's TriBeCa apartment after staying over following an evening date to see *The Hunger Games* at the cinema, followed by a visit to *Sleep No More*, an interactive art exhibition.

'They stayed as close and intimate as they could,' an insider told *Us Weekly* magazine, who also said that they perused the show 'for hours'. 'They seemed to be really enjoying each other's company,' the source added. Within hours they were back together again for lunch and shopping.

Kim has also talked about the feeling of being addicted to love and could not wait to leap into another serious relationship. She and her brother Rob are both known as the hopeless romantics in the family, and Kim has admitted she always believes she will end up marrying every man she dates! And before she met Kanye she described her ideal man as fit and healthy with a great smile and a sense of style.

She also pointed out that Kourtney is the polar opposite of the romantic daydreamer. She takes a very relaxed attitude to her love life and doesn't feel any pressure to be married, unlike Kim who has always dreamed of her ideal man pulling up on a white horse, waving a princess crown above his head for her!

In fact, Kim has admitted that the reason she cries so much is because she's a hopeless, incurable romantic. She loves the catharsis of a good cry after a really soppy love movie, rating it as the best thing in the world on certain days.

As she's grown up, the pursuit of her ideal man has become more and more of a priority to Kim. High in her wish-list are the need for her man to have a winning smile, the ability to make her laugh, and – ideally – a great sense of style (although Kim has said she could teach him if he doesn't!) But most importantly, she had always dreamed of a man who is passionate about his career – no matter what he did.

Other practical concerns include fitness, as Kim is known to have an incredibly demanding fitness regime to sculpt her curves to perfection and keep them that way. It's a part of her daily schedule and Kim knew any man she settled down with would have to be able to match that commitment. As an incredibly organised person, she craves a solid routine and plans – even to the point of planning daily itineraries on holiday.

But for Kim, the ultimate maxim she lives by is her belief that everyone comes into your life for a reason, and that you can always trust your gut when it comes to meeting a new guy for the first time. Whether it's just a casual thing, a strong shoulder to lean on or a soulmate for life, Kim maintains that everyone who has come into her life has been there for a reason and helped her grow as a person.

Meanwhile, Kim and Kanye appeared closer than ever and, finally, the couple gave the confirmation fans had been waiting for – Kanye released a new song, 'Cold', declaring his love for the reality TV star. It appeared from the lyrics that Kanye was admitting to falling for Kim when she was with her now-estranged husband Kris Humphries. He also joked about getting Jay-Z to drop Kris from the New Jersey Nets, since Jay-Z is a part owner in the team.

Days later Kim was quizzed over her relationship with Kanye on the *Today* show and while she did not openly confirm the romance, she did not deny it either.

Asked by host Ann Curry if the 'Kimye' romance was true, she giggled: 'Kanye and I have been friends for years,' before adding: 'So, I love the song,' in reference to the track 'Theraflu', which is about them falling in love.

In another sign she was ready to move on to a new relationship, when asked about her failed marriage to Humphries, Kim said defiantly: 'I'm really ready to close that chapter. I have closed that chapter. You never know what the future holds or where my life will take me.'

Humphries hit back by publicly warning Kanye that he would need a lot of patience in his relationship with Kim, and wished the rapper 'good luck'.

The source also claimed: 'Kris knows for a fact that this dalliance between Kim and Kanye has been going on for at least the last two years. Kim kept in touch with Kanye after she married Kris and promised him that she would cut off communication with him, but she never did.

'Kris is suspicious of the timing of Kim deciding to go public with the relationship because the new season of *Keeping Up With The Kardashians* is premiering in May, and Kanye has released a new album.'

According to *Radaronline.com* the rapper was even making plans to appear on the new series of Kim's reality show. A source told the website: 'Kanye is head over heels in love with Kim, and he has told her he would love to appear on the reality show if she wants him to.

'Kim is a bit leery of having her man appear on camera because of the whole fiasco with her soon-to-be-ex-husband Kris Humphries, but watch for Kanye to make several appearances on the show towards the end of the season.'

However the *Huffington Post* threw that into doubt when it reported that all 18 episodes of the new show had already been filmed, having been shot before Kim and Kanye officially got together.

Kim's sister Khloe was also quizzed about the romance when she appeared on *The Ellen DeGeneres Show* and was asked by the chatshow host if the rumours were true. And Khloe certainly added fuel to the fire with her hints, but did not openly admit that the superstar pair were actually dating. She said: 'Honestly, we've known Kanye forever. He's been a great family friend. I love Kanye.

'I don't know what happens with Kim. I think they are cute together. I've said that, but honey, I don't know. You've got to get her on the show and ask her.'

Khloe tried unsuccessfully to change the subject, but added: 'I like Kanye. I think Kim and Kanye, they've known each other for a really long time, and they're good friends.

'They're compatible. I think friendship is where good relationships stem from.'

The pair then discussed Kim's impending divorce and Khloe revealed that she was the only person who had warned Kim that marrying Humphries might be a bad move: 'I don't know why no one else told her that,' Khloe said. 'She got mad at me. I like being honest. I like Kris as a person. I just did not like them together.'

On another American TV show, called *Watch What Happens Live*, Khloe revealed a little more about her sister's new romance: 'I don't think it's serious. I think it's too soon. But because they've been friends for so long, it's just so easy and that's something I love seeing for Kim – the easiness and how happy she is.

'It's just more of a great friendship and friendships make the best relationships. We've known Kanye for, like, nine years. He's great with the family, but again we've known him for so long. It's not like some stranger getting into a hurricane.'

But it was becoming increasingly difficult for the couple to remain coy when they were spotted on another dinner date at one of New York City's hottest restaurants, Spice Market, a trendy Asian Fusion spot in the city's Meatpacking District. It also emerged that Kim had introduced her new man to her family on the very same day, a sure sign things were gradually becoming more serious.

And according to showbiz website *TMZ*, the Kardashian crew 'absolutely loved him'. A source said: 'Kanye and Kim were excited for the family gathering and the opportunity to show them just how great they are together. The meeting went great and the family thinks they make the perfect couple.'

But just as their romance was starting to flourish – Kim had even been spotted wearing earrings featuring Kanye's initials – the pair came under fire. *Mad Men* actor Jon Hamm publicly branded Kim a 'f***ing idiot', adding the lure of celebrity made people like Kim and her former best friend Paris Hilton into millionaires for no good reason, and when he had the opportunity to backtrack on his harsh statements, he refused.

Hamm told *Today* show host Matt Lauer: 'I don't think [my comments] were careless. I think they were accurate.' Kim took to her Twitter page to express her feelings on the matter. She wrote: 'Calling someone who runs their own businesses, is a part of a successful TV show, produces, writes, designs, and creates, "stupid," is in my opinion careless.

'I respect Jon and I am a firm believer that everyone is entitled to their own opinion and that not everyone takes the same path in life. We're all working hard and we all have to respect one another.'

Kim meanwhile had fallen out with Paris Hilton in a public spat. As Kim shot to fame, Paris started to take shots at her, even calling Kim's bottom 'gross' and adding: 'It reminds me of cottage cheese inside a big trash bag.'

The criticism did not seem to dent Kim's star power, however. Just days later she was invited to dine with President Barack Obama at The White House Correspondents' dinner in Washington, and admitted she was thrilled to be invited to such a glamorous event. She recalled panicking after a last minute invite and realising she had nothing to wear. In the end, Kris volunteered a Valentino dress she got in Paris in 1984, which turned out to be a perfect fit – she apparently even cried when she saw how nice it looked!

The flashbulbs exploded when Kim arrived, and she later revealed her secrets for posing on the red carpet: 'Take the time to look in the mirror to see the way you look best. Suck it in, have great posture, stick your booty out!'

CHAPTER 4

HEATING UP

The future was most definitely starting to look bright for Kim and Kanye by the spring of 2012, they were photographed hand in hand almost every day, and yet there was one fly in the ointment. Kim was technically still married and had to endure her impending divorce proceedings with Kris Humphries. Kim hired the best legal help in the business, lawyer-to-the-stars Laura Wasser, and it emerged that Kim had been spending hours in meetings at the lawyer's home.

Reportedly, Kris wanted his former wife to tell the truth, the whole truth and nothing but the truth and admit that the real reason she married him, at least as far as he was concerned, was for publicity. But during the first brief court hearing Wasser turned the tables and accused Humphries of attempting to prolong the proceedings to dissolve their marriage for publicity's sake. But the NBA player refused to be intimidated, and said the only way he could be persuaded not to take the case to a trial would be if Kim publicly apologised to him, and admitted that she only married him to boost her television ratings.

'Kris just wants the truth to come out and Kim is just absolutely livid that she isn't getting her own way,' a source told *Radar Online*. 'Kris wants Kim to answer questions about their relationship, under oath. Kris is ready for a fight and he has said that Kim should "bring it on".

'Kris won't be silenced and he isn't after her money, he doesn't want one dime from her. It's just about the truth coming out, something that Kim's camp seems to be petrified about.'

As part of the proceedings, the Brooklyn Nets player was demanding to know what had happened to one of their more lavish wedding presents, a $325,000 white Ferrari, which was given to them by a wealthy Malaysian businessman.

Meanwhile Kim added fuel to the fire the same week when she tweeted her approval of a radio show that was publicly criticising the six-foot-nine-inch ball player.

The hosts of the *Cipha Sounds and Rosenberg* radio show on Hot 97 said how much they approved of Kim's new boyfriend and called Humphries a 'nobody' on the air.

'He went from being an unknown NBA player to one of the most talked about players, just because of dating Kim,' said Rosenberg, adding: 'He even became a better basketball player after dating and marrying her.'

Kim, who has over 21 million Twitter followers and is among the most-followed people on Instagram, immediately took to her Twitter page to comment. She wrote: 'Was listening to Hot 97 this morning! Thanks for the shout out lol! I love those guys!!!'

Kris was the one who filed for the divorce, less than three months after their wedding, and when the trial was due to begin his legal team argued that they needed more time to gather information.

And while the legal wrangling rumbled on, Kim was determined to prove her cool credentials in trying to get herself invited to the fashion event of the year. But she was left off the guest list for the famous Metropolitan Museum of Art Costume Institute Gala in 2012, allegedly because of a rift with *US Vogue* editor-in-chief Anna Wintour, who hosts the glitzy bash every year.

While stars including Gwyneth Paltrow, Heidi Klum and Emma Stone lapped up the attention on the red carpet, Kim was left out in the cold, tweeting her way through the prestigious event from home. She even posted a blog discussing the best-dressed celebrities from the night. Even more surprising was that Kanye was on the guest list, and strutted up the red carpet with his friend Jay-Z and his pop star wife Beyoncé.

A source told *Radar Online* that the powerful magazine editor excluded Kim because she was not a fan of *Keeping Up With The Kardashians*: 'Why would she be invited to the event? It is all the biggest stars in the world and Kim doesn't fit that bill at all.

'She would have done anything to be there with all the A-listers' the source added.

After the Gala, Kim vowed to be more private. Although

she had shared almost every aspect of her life with the cameras in recent years, she planned not to 'over-share' about her new relationship.

Khloe's reality show, *Khloe and Lamar*, had documented a series of intimate moments in her marriage to Lamar Odom, and Kim was determined not to follow suit, even though she confirmed that Kanye would at some stage appear in *Keeping Up With The Kardashians*.

'I'm not going to be taking a bubble bath and drinking champagne or on a sex swing [on camera] like Khloe and Lamar do,' Kim told *E! News*. 'It's not going to be like that.

'I want to show my life. If we are having dinner and he does show up, I'm sure we're not going to go, "Stop the cameras!"'

She admitted that she had learnt her lesson after the very public breakdown of her marriage to Kris: 'My heart's a little more guarded,' she said. 'I showed so much of myself in the past. You almost get embarrassed showing this big wedding [...] So I think you want to just guard yourself.'

However, Kim and Kanye continued to be inseparable, and they were filmed at a LA Lakers basketball game together. Afterwards Khloe told Kourtney: 'Kanye and Kim, they are kind of like two peas in a pod.'

They then jetted out to France, where the couple made a splash at the Cannes Film Festival. Kim wanted to support Kanye at the premiere of his new short film, *Cruel Summer*, and they spent most of their time on the French Riviera kissing and wrapping their arms around each other.

And while at the festival Kim finally made up with her rival and former best friend Paris Hilton after they shared a touching heart-to-heart. They had been feuding ever since Kim outgrew the lowly role of the socialite's stylist to top the reality television tree with her own show. But they had a deep conversation together at the amfAR gala at the Hotel du Cap-Eden-Roc in Antibes. According to the *New York Post*, witnesses were amazed to see them all smiles during their chance meeting. One witness said they had 'hugged, smiled and chatted for a while'.

The source added: 'They really have no problem with each other; it has been a long time.'

However, Kim's happiness was short-lived after she and Kanye travelled on to London for a whistle-stop promotional tour, only to discover that her luggage had been rifled through. Kim said that 'irreplaceable' items had been stolen from her suitcases and that her visit to Europe had ended on a sour note after 'sentimental' items were removed from her suitcase.

She fired off a series of angry tweets, saying: 'What happened to the days when you could lock your bags! We need to get back to that. There's no sense of security & no trust! Shame on you.'

To add to matters, it emerged around the same time that her ex-husband had found himself a new girlfriend and with her curvy figure, clinging dresses and long dark hair, there was no getting away from the comparisons between Kim and Fatmire Sinanaj, known as Myla.

Five years younger than Kim, Myla appeared smitten with Kris as they were photographed together everywhere from the beaches of Miami to New York hotels, and she was regularly courtside at his basketball matches. Despite their obvious happiness, Myla could not resist taking a swipe at Kim's family and wrote on Twitter that Kim's stepdad Bruce Jenner's face 'scares me', adding: 'It should be on the "Why not to get plastic surgery" poster.'

But regardless of the barbs and criticisms they faced from all sides, Kim and Kanye were determined to move forward with their relationship. And as a sign of his commitment, Kanye put his $4million home on the market so they could live together. It did not take long for the unusual four-bedroom and four-bathroom house in the heart of Los Angeles to be snapped up.

Boasting a life-size Buzz Lightyear figurine among other expensive toys, the eye-popping décor was homage to kitsch pop culture, with artworks of iconic American cartoon family The Jetsons adorning the walls, Andy Warhol's 'Campbell's Soup can' paintings, and huge piles of stuffed animals.

Despite his hip-hop swagger, West's home was in fact the furthest thing imaginable from the cool properties often featured on shows such as *MTV Cribs*. Built on spec, the 4,200-square-foot, three-level house started out as a beige stucco monolith, which the rapper transformed over three years with the help of interior designer Don Stewart into what he described as 'a cross between a museum and a Louis Vuitton boutique.' After installing walnut flooring, and opening up the space for a loft-like feel, he commissioned a series of six Jetsons' portraits, to accompany the game room's chair of stuffed animals by Fernando and Humberto Campana and a Smurf-blue 'Igloo' armchair by Eero Koivisto.

Nestled high in the Hollywood Hills, Kanye also gave the

guest room a retro touch, thanks to a 1970s desk in white acrylic, which reflected pink from a fuchsia silk-screen Marilyn set behind it. But Kanye saved the real glamour for his master bedroom. The suite featured an Antonio Citterio bed draped with red fox and chinchilla throws.

Being a dedicated follower of fashion, Kanye's wardrobe was enormous, with 8-foot-high sliding racks for almost 200 pairs of trainers.

Of course, Kim could not contain her excitement at the progress of their relationship, although in a TV interview with chat show queen Oprah Winfrey she tried to claim that she preferred not to talk about it: 'In the past I suffered a lot because of my honesty, and when it didn't work I was criticised and treated badly. I can only say that now, with him, I'm happy,' she said. 'Everyone is always watching me. I'm under constant observation, everywhere I go there's a camera following me, in the gym, when I do the shopping, and if I decide to go out without make-up it makes news throughout the world.'

But Kim absolutely was clear that marriage to Humphries was not a hoax and that she was left utterly depressed after the romance failed, and her fan-base was strong enough without having to stage drama for ratings.

In an extremely frank interview with Winfrey she stressed that she still has a 'place in my heart' for Kris, yet after moving in together it dawned on her that married life was 'not for me'.

'I was in love, I wanted the life that I always pictured my fairy tale life to be,' Kim explained. 'I would have had an extravagant wedding anyway, to end that relationship was a risk in itself to lose ratings and I had to take the risk to be honest to myself.'

Although she never mentioned Kris by name throughout the interview, Kim claimed that the pair had not spent enough time alone before their wedding for her to recognise their incompatibility.

She continued: 'I think when people first meet, everything is great in the beginning, but I didn't spend more than a whole week with my ex before we married.

'When we moved in together, I saw how our relationship was. I don't want to get into the small things, but once we moved in, I knew he was not the one.'

Oprah quizzed her about pre-wedding nerves, and Kim said: 'I didn't have an inkling, but everyone around me did. The night before, Mom said, "Do you want out?" She said, "You're not yourself." But I said no. I got angry, I was thinking, "How dare you!"'

Kim stressed that Kris did not do anything specifically wrong. 'He's a good person,' she added. 'I will always have a place in my heart for him. It just wasn't for me.'

While Kim admitted she was 'bored', she did not say this was the reason she left Kris: 'You know in your heart,' she said. 'Mom was supportive, so I took that time off afterwards. I would rather have been beaten up in the media than live a life that wasn't happy.

'I was in such a deep depression I thought I was going to back away from everything. I stayed at home for almost four months and I'm a better person now, as heartbreaking as it was to go through. For anyone I hurt, I'm truly sorry. I don't wish pain on anyone, but the person I am because of that crazy experience, I wouldn't change it for the world.

'I loved him, obviously it hurt him, and it hurt me too. It was embarrassing. I don't want to call it a mistake, it was a lesson.'

In the interview, which was watched by a global audience of millions, Kim went on to knock back accusations that she only became famous in the wake of a sex tape scandal. Five years since the controversial tape of Kim and ex-boyfriend Ray J was released, she said that she understood the impact it had had on her career: 'Would you be where you are had there not been a sex tape?' Oprah asked Kim, who admitted: 'You know, I think that's how I was definitely introduced to the world. It was a negative way, so I felt like I really had to work ten times harder to get people to see the real me.'

The sex tape was the focus of a lawsuit, which she finally settled with Vivid Entertainment.

She went on: 'Yes, I was born rich; it was a classic Californian lineage: lavishness and ostentation, luxury mansions with pools, private clubs, exclusive friendships, and luxury cars.

'Despite the affluence, I've been able to build my own empire in the world of entertainment and, although looks and friendships are important, I want the new generation to understand that if you don't believe in yourself and in your own ideas, you go nowhere.'

Indeed Kim has worked hard to build her business empire, which has seen her endorse everything from cupcakes and lollipops to jewellery and jeans. Her attempts at acting and singing have backfired, however, with one critic from the *New*

York Daily News blasting her single 'Jam': 'A dead-brained piece of generic dance music, without a single distinguishing feature performed by the worst singer in the reality TV universe.'

During the two-part interview with Oprah, Kim went on to explain how splitting from Kris and getting together with Kanye, who is four years older than her, had changed her as a person: 'It's like how Kourtney had this epiphany when she had her baby and she changed into a different person. I feel like I've had an epiphany over the last year.

'For what I've been through and I am that changed person, just from my own experiences.

'I always dated five years younger. My whole thing was completely different, and now I just love that I'm with someone that's a couple years older than me.' In fact, Kim confessed, she was so in love with Kanye she had just splashed out $400,000 on a sleek Lamborghini for his thirty-fifth birthday.

During the interview Kim said that as an Armenian she felt proud to represent Middle Eastern women in modern society. And when asked by Oprah if she thought the Kardashians' reality TV show would be as successful if they weren't pretty, she replied: 'I don't think it would have happened if we were all skinny pretty models.

'I think it has to do with us, the curves, the dark hair – I think it was a combination.

'I remember when the wave of Jennifer Lopez, Salma Hayek and these beautiful Hispanic women came into light, and I looked up to them and I loved them, but I was like, "Where are Middle Eastern women?" I think we took that category or helped broaden that.'

There were even more revelations in store when Kim left the audience stunned after disclosing that her mother had put her on birth control pills at the tender age of fourteen.

Kim told Oprah she was 'almost fifteen' when her mother Kris made the bold move, as a result of her desire to lose her virginity to her boyfriend of two years.

Kim said: 'When I did want to have sex the first time I was almost fifteen. I was like, "I think I'm going to, or I want to," and she was like, "Okay, so this is what we're gonna do, we're gonna put you on birth control," and she was really open and honest with me.'

The revelation came as a surprise to the veteran broadcaster Oprah, who simply said: 'Wow!' before moving swiftly onto the next question.

But Kris admitted she felt no hesitation in putting 'all' of her girls on the birth control pill as soon as they expressed an interest in sex. 'You want to protect your kids,' she said afterwards. 'Kim came to me and you know, was very honest with me and said, "Mummy, I think I'm feeling, you know, sexual."

'What I did as a parent with all my girls, when I felt like it was that time in their life that they were going to that step, I drove as fast as I could to the gynaecologist's office,' she continued. 'You can try and talk your kids out of [having sex], but unless you lock your child in the closet and throw the key away, they're going to do what they feel.

'So my philosophy has also been make sure your kids are healthy, well taken care of and educated.'

She added that the doctor who gave all her daughters birth control was the same one who had delivered them as babies.

Kim certainly seemed determined to convince the world that she was more normal than she appeared but writing in *The Sunday Times Magazine*, she revealed that she still lived in a privileged bubble, having all her food delivered in special packs which she kept in the fridge, although she went on to claim that despite having a cleaner she insists on doing all her housework herself: 'My food is delivered every day in little freezer packs, I put those in the refrigerator and make sure it's all tidy,' she wrote. 'I can't take a shower unless the bathroom is absolutely spotless. I think I'm totally OCD, everything has to be immaculate. I have a cleaner who comes three times a week but I always do the cleaning on top of that.'

Although she appeared to have her life very much in order, Kim was already making plans to start a family, with or without Kanye. In an episode of *Keeping Up With The Kardashians*, she made a startling revelation to her sister Kourtney: 'If I'm forty and not married, I would have a baby artificially inseminated,' she said.

Meanwhile Kim found herself under fire yet again when a British headmistress singled her out as an example of all that is wrong with Western society. Dr Helen Wright, the head of St Mary's School, an exclusive girls' boarding school in Wiltshire, made her claim after one men's magazine branded Miss Kardashian 'the hottest woman in the world'.

A fuming Dr Wright said: 'The hottest woman in the world? Really? Is this what we want our young people to aim for? Is this what success should mean to them?'

At the same time Kim was also being sued by a group of New York women who had launched a £3million lawsuit against her and her sister, Kourtney, for endorsing diet pills. The siblings appeared in billboard adverts for QuickTrim, under the slogan, 'Burn it up, flush it out', and claimed that their enviable figures were due to the pills. However, the disgruntled customers claim that, as the pills contain only caffeine, this could not be possible. The sisters managed to successfully fight the lawsuit.

On top of the TV work, Kim was also raking in the cash from her chain of fashion boutiques, Dash, as well as the cheaper range, K Dash, which was sold on the home shopping TV channel QVC. She was also endorsing Sketchers body-toning trainers and Kotex panty liners. Sales of her namesake perfume earned her £4million, not to mention a range of swimwear called Beach Bunny and a workout video that goes under the title of *Fit In Your Jeans by Friday*.

On top of that, for a £7,000 fee she was prepared to tweet about products to her many millions of followers on Twitter.

Kim defended her business decisions; she has told how her parents always encouraged their children to work hard, to take their business interests seriously – and not to simply accept every endorsement opportunity that comes their way.

Despite the constant barrage of criticism, her romance with Kanye continued to flourish. And although she had pledged to keep her private life to herself, Kim could not help gushing about how well they were getting along. She told how Kanye 'knows everything' about her.

Kim explained how Kanye met the criteria she and her sisters demanded of all potential partners. All the girls like men who can make them laugh and keep them entertained, they also insist on being friends so they can talk to him and count on him through life's ups and downs. They also demand respect and monogamy, and have said how the test of a good relationship is whether they can be happy at home doing absolutely nothing together!

Kim also said in an *Oprah* interview that she was finding her relationship with the rapper – who was left devastated after his mother Donda died from complications following cosmetic surgery in 2007 – 'comforting' because they could relate to each other's life experiences. Kim, whose father Robert died of cancer in 2003, said in a 2012 interview with Oprah Winfrey: 'It's very comforting to have someone that knows everything about you, that respects you, understands, has gone through the similar things. I can really relate to his mother passing.

'He can really relate to my father passing. I mean, there's so many similarities in our life that I feel like I'm at a really happy, good space.' She also admitted in the same interview that she had been friends with Kanye for 'six or seven years' before they started dating.

And she said her previous experiences helped their relationship: 'I don't know why it took so long for us to get together, but I think I needed to go through all my experiences.

'I think we've always had an attraction to each other but we've always been in other relationships or it wasn't the right timing. And one day it just happened. It took me by surprise,' she explained.

And she denied that she and Kanye were only together for publicity: 'It's your heart you're playing with. I couldn't sacrifice my heart for a publicity stunt,' she said. 'But I think having him in my life right now, in this way, says so much about us.

'I want babies; I want my forever; I want my fairy tale. And I believe you can have what you want.'

Kim also admitted that being in the glare of the public eye was taking its toll as she felt under constant pressure to always look her very best. But she was reluctant to describe herself as 'beautiful', as she explained: 'I hate to talk about myself like that. I'm so critical.

'But I do feel pretty. It is a job. Gym every day. I've lasered everything. But now what makes me happy in life doesn't have to do with "all the way" me – if that makes sense.'

As well as facing relentless criticism over her appearance, Kim was also coming under fire for her unlikely friendship with Beyoncé. Following pictures of the pair watching their men perform together during their joint 'Watch The Throne' concert tour, fans of the Grammy award-winning singer said they were unimpressed with her rubbing shoulders with the reality star.

'Beyoncé tries to stay out of the tabloids, while they're Kim's livelihood,' an insider told Radar Online. 'It's an odd pairing.'

Kim was careful not to comment on her new friend, and a source told the *New York Daily News* that she was playing her cards very carefully in order to gain Beyoncé's trust: 'She's hung with them a few times already, but she isn't saying peep about them. She's not tweeting or taking pictures with Beyoncé because she doesn't want to seem desperate.'

According to reports, the two women dined together before attending the show at the LG Arena in Birmingham, at a meal arranged by Kanye in a bid to bring them closer together. A source told *The Sun* newspaper: 'The girls have never really seen eye-to-eye. It's a shame because Jay-Z and Kanye are so close. Beyoncé has always viewed Kim as a reality TV star who's not earned her fortune with a specific talent.

'Kanye arranged a dinner in the hotel suite for the girls to clear the air. He's hoping that now they're pals it will lead to further get-togethers away from the tour. Beyoncé has now welcomed Kim into the clan.'

Beyoncé was spotted in the crowd the following night at the Hackney Weekend festival when Jay-Z and Kanye performed together again, but it was not known if Kim was there too.

In a magazine interview just days later Kim said she did not care what people thought of her relationship with Kanye, especially if they suspected some of his lyrics were about her.

'People can interpret it however they want. That's him making music,' she told *InStyle* magazine. 'We know what we are to each other. We've had a deep friendship for so long and that's the start of a really good relationship.'

She also went on to reveal that she had learnt lessons about love from her high-profile divorce from Kris Humphries: 'I loved this person, it just wasn't the right situation for me.

'I've always been the type to fall in love fast and, with every boyfriend I plan out my wedding in my head. It's taught me to take things slow. I've always believed in love. I haven't always been so lucky, but I still do believe in it.'

Ever the optimist, she added that she was hopeful about starting a family with Kanye too. She said: 'If you had asked me that a year ago, I would have said no, but things change. Now, I think I would.

'I want to be married with two parents in the house to raise the kids. But, if that wasn't the option for me, I would do it on my own.

'If you're a Kardashian you simply cannot have a relationship without everyone in the whole family being part of it. All of us are so close and involved in each other's lives that it's impossible to avoid. We're very protective of each other. 'But sometimes it can get out of control!'

Luckily for Kanye, Kim's sisters adored him immediately, and he was quickly accepted into the clan.

For all her curves, reality television appearances and high-profile public appearances, Kim had never been taken seriously for her fashion sense. But that was all set to change soon after she got together with Kanye. Since first appearing on TV in 2007 she had mostly chosen colourful dresses, micro-miniskirts and cleavage baring, low-cut tops. But when she and Kanye jetted off to Paris Haute Couture Fashion Week in the spring of 2013, she displayed a selection of carefully curated high-fashion ensembles.

Reminiscent of Victoria Beckham's fashion overhaul after leaving the Spice Girls, easily one of the most seamless celebrity career and style transitions recorded, Kim successfully said goodbye to her cleavage and embraced her curves with an entirely new demure but sexy wardrobe. Although her pout, heavy mascara and voluptuous figure remained intact, gone were the bright colours, plunging necklines, curled hair extensions and leopard print platform heels.

Seemingly determined to prove she was taking fashion seriously, she showcased a subdued, but punchy monochrome palette, with collarbone skimming necklines and her hair was suddenly sleek and straight, pulled back or classically middle-parted. Of course she continued to showcase her hourglass figure in outfits that clung to her hips and bust too, but now she started to team them with long-sleeves and high-waisted skirts that fell below her knees. She began to favour soft leather over nylon, streamlined stilettos over chunky platforms and Kayne West's Nike 'Air Yeezy' sneakers over thigh-high boots.

As well as sitting front row at both the Stéphane Rolland and Givenchy couture shows in Paris, she also defied her critics by landing her first *Vogue* cover, for the July–August issue of Italy's *L'Uomo Vogue*. While it may not have been front-row at Chanel, or the holy-grail of *Vogue* covers, Anna Wintour's American edition, with each step Kim was leaving her over-the-top days behind her, keeping fans glued to her Instagram feed as they watched her transformation from Jersey Shore to Paris couture.

Clearly focused on keeping up with Kanye in the fashion stakes, it emerged that Kim had been asking him for daily advice on what to wear, and when he made his debut appearance on her family's show she was seen seeking his opinion on what jewellery to wear with her little black dress. She also asked for his thoughts on what handbag to carry to brother-in-law Scott Disick's restaurant opening: 'Don't you think this clutch is too busy for this?' she asks him.

In May a source told *The Sun* newspaper: 'Kanye has been having chats with Kim about her style. He thinks she should be more like him, edgy with her choices. He keeps saying she should "evolve" as a fashion icon.

'Kanye says she plays it safe too much so has been trying to pick outfits for her to wear and encourage her to be more daring.'

Kim's transformation was seen by many as a sign that their relationship was moving on to the next level, and rumours began to swirl that an engagement was on the cards: 'They're seriously talking marriage. And yes, she would [accept his proposal],' a source close to the couple told *Us Weekly* magazine. 'Kanye says he can't wait to see her carrying his child. He says she will look beautiful pregnant.'

Around the same time Kim was seen driving Kanye's $750,000 Lamborghini sports car, and proudly wearing a pair of earrings with the initials KW, but she refused to put a 'title' on their relationship. In footage from her TV show, Khloe appeared concerned that her sister was rushing into another serious romance too fast, telling her: 'I think Kim wants to believe that she can take things slow,' Khloe says. 'But let's keep it real – you're wearing KW earrings, I know what that stands for.'

Kim told her: 'I don't want to make a big fuss about it – we're just hanging out.' But it then emerged that Kanye had asked a private jeweller to craft a piece for his girlfriend using diamond earrings and a ruby ring from his late mother Donda's personal collection as he was planning to propose when her divorce to Humphries became finalised.

'Donda was such an important person in Kanye's life, he thought the world of her and was devastated when she died,' revealed a source close to the rapper. 'So, he kept all her jewellery as keepsakes – a lot of the pieces were items he bought over the years after he made it as a hip-hop star.

'And now, Kanye has found a woman he respects and loves just as much as his mom, so he wants to share her jewellery collection with Kim.'

The source went on to tell *Radar Online* that Kanye hoped to marry Kim either in Chicago, where he was raised, or Oklahoma, where Donda is buried: 'Kanye is an emotional character and has earmarked Chicago or Oklahoma as the two places he'd love to wed Kim.'

However, friends apparently advised Kanye against having a one-of-a-kind engagement ring made for he would struggle to get the precious jewels back if he and Kim were to split. The source explained: 'His friends think it's a terrible idea and are advising him not to give Kim the ring. Because it's a gift, it would be difficult for Kanye to ask for it back if they ever split up.'

Despite the warnings, just days later the couple were spotted sporting similar gold bracelets as they enjoyed a drink in New York, and Kim tweeted a photo of their arms with the caption 'His & Hers'.

The wedding rumours intensified when Kim suddenly vowed to lose weight, shortly after being subjected to a barrage of abuse on Twitter about her figure:

According to the website *EntertainmentWise* 'I used to eat a ton of junk food, but there are plenty of fast food places that offer healthy options, so there's no excuse for eating badly all the time,' she said. 'Although, when I go out for dinner, I eat what I want. You can't spend your life worrying about calories.'

And she went on to reveal that she had found the perfect way to slim down – the sex diet! Kim had always been one to jump on the latest diet bandwagon, whether it was working up a sweat at boot camp or promoting a slimming shake. But as she showed off her beach-ready curves during a break to Miami, it emerged that she had honed them with the help of her boyfriend: 'We jokingly refer to it as the sex diet,' a close friend told the *National Enquirer*. 'When one of us is having regular sex, that tends to burn calories and kill the appetite. Losing seven pounds in seven days means being a very naughty girl.'

According to the same source, however, Kanye prefers her more natural shape: 'Kanye loves her curves and has told her repeatedly that she shouldn't get too skinny. He's always encouraging her just to be happy and healthy and do things for herself and not give in to peer pressure, which is why he doesn't think she should lose weight.

'Kim was speechless, especially when he told her he missed her love handles. Kanye can't understand why she has lost weight when she knows it's not the look he likes.

'He thinks Kim should be doing everything to please him – not herself.'

But Kim has made a career out of looking good, and so she continued with her exercise and beauty regime, which she has described as a full-time job. Most days she would treat her millions of Twitter followers to daily snaps of herself working out and being pampered as it was revealed that the cost of looking like Kim Kardashian was a staggering £66,000 a year – and that was without all the freebies the star received for endorsing armfuls of products, including OPI nail polish, Illumifill line-filling make-up and, of course, the QuickTrim diet supplement.

According to *Heat* magazine she would splash out on at least £5,500 of treatments every month, spending over 180 hours beautifying herself with fortnightly £800 facials at Beverly Hills salon Bailey's, as well as a monthly 24-carat gold UMO facials and twice-weekly anti-ageing glycolic facial peels. Kim is also huge fan of permanent eyelash extensions and has a weekly appointment to fix any strays and keep them topped up.

Regular blasts of Fraxel cosmetic laser treatment, costing up to £2,000 a time, keep her complexion peachy and twice-monthly spa days at the five-star Four Seasons hotel keep her body in top condition. Her favourite treatments include £110 body scrubs made with tequila, tangerine and sunflower oil.

She has admitted to having laser cellulite removal on various parts of her body, and two detoxifying mud wraps per month keep her skin flawless. Kim spends an hour a day on either a massage, skin and nail treatments. A nail session at Beverly Hills Nail Design sets her back £95 a time.

The brunette goes to celebrity stylist Philip Wolff at the Shades salon in Beverly Hills for £500 styling sessions to keep her sew-in weft extensions in tip-top condition. Kim also treats them at home with an hour-long conditioning treatment.

And on top of all that she works out every day with celebrity trainer Gunnar Peterson, who has said: 'Kim is an incredibly hard worker. She comes right from the airport to the gym and is no stranger to 6am workouts.'

Kim explained in her book *Kardashian Kondfidential* how she likes to mix up her workouts with legendary trainer Gunnar, the man who whipped the cast of muscle-bound action flick *The Expendables* into peak shape. To keep her legs toned and strong she switches between squats, lunges and weighted exercises, and keeps her cardio ticking over with a gruelling Barry's Bootcamp session.

As a post-workout snack, she tucks into a healthy smoothie packed with bananas and peanut butter, sometimes supplementing it with a breakfast of scrambed egg whites, turkey bacon, mushrooms and tomatoes. Lunches and dinners usually revolve around a lean diet of chicken and salad.

But everyone needs a treat now and again, and for Kim a cheeseburger and fries, or a homemade vanilla cake, can't be beaten – except perhaps by the artichoke dip at The Cheesecake Factory! But Kim notes that she doesn't really drink, except for the odd glass of wine on a special occasion. Never mind alcohol - the biggest vice she has is cookies and cream!

She has also been vocal on the subject of body image, saying that whilst she tends to prefer her body when it's on thinner side, her curves mean she'll never be a stick-figure and that's okay by her. She doesn't feel the need to deprive herself or starve to achieve the unrealistically thin bodies some models sport.

Citing a couple of girls in high school she knew, she said that they were obsessed with their weight and actually went on to develop eating disorders through intensive crash-course dieting. They'd try to give her tips and Kim couldn't believe the things they were putting themselves through to lose the extra pounds.

Kim has said that she hopes young girls would look at her and her sisters and realise that each one has a different natural body shape, but that they all felt comfortable - and desirable – with their own bodies.

Indeed, to show his appreciation for his curvy lady, Kanye wrote a new song in August 2012 called 'Perfect Bitch', in tribute to his glamorous girlfriend. In the song he rapped about his search for the ideal woman and how he has now found the 'perfect bitch'. But rival rapper 50 Cent kicked off a new feud with his old sparring partner. He told *XXL* magazine: 'You know how it is? One man's trash is another man's treasure. I mean, if that man feel like she's perfect, then she's perfect.

'He could mean it and you'll end up singing the words to it because he's Kanye. I'm not sure. The smartest guys I know have lost being a bad judge of character in that area.' Kanye had always tried to ignore the criticism levelled at him by 50 Cent, who has also lashed out at his friends Jay-Z and Beyoncé.

Throughout his career 50 Cent has been a rival of Kanye's, and in 2007 he famously promised to quit music if his *Curtis* album was outsold by Kanye's third studio album, *Graduation*. Of course the latter went on to top the charts after selling 957,000 copies in the first week, while 50 Cent took the number two spot, selling 691,000 units. Despite his previous assertions, 50 Cent continued in the industry, and has gone on to release several more albums.

CHAPTER 5

CLEARING THE WAY FOR MARRIAGE

Although it took them both a while to admit it openly, things between Kim and Kanye were getting serious pretty fast, and Kim could not help revealing the true extent of her feelings for her man, and eventually admitted that she felt he was 'the one' and was busy plotting spending the rest of their lives together.

In a revealing interview with *New York* magazine, she told how she sees them both in their old age, simply enjoying each other's company: 'When this whole life is done, and it's just the two of us sitting somewhere when we're 80, you want to have things to talk about that you have in common.'

She added: 'I think that's something maybe I didn't value as highly as a quality I cared about in someone.'

Among the 'things' that the pair clearly had in common was a shared passion for fashion, as it was revealed in the same week that Kanye had presented Kim with a $6,000 pair of shoes he had designed himself, decorated with strands of pearls.

In a 2012 interview with *New York* Magazine, Kim said 'If I have a design meeting, or he has one, we come back and talk about how our meetings went,' she went on. 'It's cool, because you can definitely get more in-depth with someone who actually knows what you're talking about.

'So that's been a fun similarity we have. I think it's essential to have similarities.'

Kim went on to explain that since meeting Kanye she had started drinking, having previously refused all alcohol, claiming she needed to 'lighten up'.

And in a further public declaration of love, Kim managed to wiggle her way into one of Kanye's music videos. The song combined Khaled's 'I Wish You Would' with Kanye's 'Cold', originally called 'Theraflu', and the lyrics implied that he could have Kim's ex, Kris Humphries, fired from the New York Jets. Meanwhile Khaled warned when the collaboration was released to expect a 'monstrous earthquake to hit the streets.'

But Kanye's friend Jay-Z, who is a part owner of the team, never made a move against Humphries. And yet, when the divorce hearing began a few weeks later, Humphries' lawyer tried to compel Kanye West to come to court – by putting a subpoena in a box from department store Nordstrom and sending it to Kim's house.

At the time Kris was still refusing to accept Kim's deposition. Kim's lawyer told a judge about Humphries' tactics, in sending the subpoena in a box. Californian law states that a subpoena must be served in person, not in the mail, meaning Kris's lawyer had apparently not followed the correct protocol. A judge has the power to fine, jail or issue a warrant for arrest to anyone who does not attend court when subpoenaed.

The NBA star also issued Kim's mother Kris Jenner with a subpoena, as well as NBC Universal and Bunim/Murray, makers of the Kardashian reality shows, in a bid to prove the marriage was a fraud to boost ratings.

Though Kris refused to settle he had signed an ironclad prenuptial agreement – meaning he had no claim on Kim's fortune – however, he did make money from his appearance on *Keeping Up With The Kardashians*.

Kim went on to post a series of intimate pictures of herself and Kanye online to show how happy the two of them were. But she admitted it can be tough dealing with the relentless public scrutiny of their relationship. In her book *Kardashian Konfidential* she said that being in a relationship in the public eye can feel like everyone (or perhaps, more accurately, the media) has to know all of your business at all times.

She points out that whilst most people are fretting about over-inquisitive mothers poking their noses in, high-profile celebrities experience the same sensation on a global scale, which can make it much harder to trust people.

But she is philosophical on the subject, acknowledging that whilst the relentless glare of the public eye can become a burden, she has learned to live with it and filter out all the nonsense which comes her way. She credits the experience of growing up in a high-profile family in helping her to learn how to keep things private and deal with the fallout from a public break-up.

Determined to prove their happiness, the couple went on to release personal footage of Kanye taking issue with some of the more questionable outfits in his girlfriend's wardrobe – even offering to buy her a new rack of clothes if she threw the old ones away.

She went on to donate almost 100 pairs of shoes, with a colour to match any outfit, to charity because Kanye had dismissed her wardrobe as 'ghetto'.

By the end of the scene the bed was heaped with piles of unwanted designer clothes, many unworn, while dozens of pairs of shoes were stacked outside Kim's room. Many looked to be brand new, perhaps worn only once or twice.

The clothes rails were bare, once Kanye had finished attaching tags to items he deemed unworthy – almost every item Kim owned was eventually tagged.

Despite previously having worked as a fashion stylist, Kim happily allowed her lover to decide which items stayed, and which were rejected. Even a fur-lined Louis Vuitton bag, which she admitted sheepishly that she was keeping for any future daughter to inherit, was consigned to the reject pile.

'Shouldn't I just keep this for, like, my daughter one day?' she asked. But Kanye failed to appreciate her hints that they might one day have a family, instead remaining pointedly silent.

When Kim told her sister Khloe that Kanye had labelled her wardrobe 'ghetto', Khloe was outraged: 'You gotta have a little ghetto in your life!' she squealed.

Luckily Kanye declared himself delighted with his girlfriend's 'magazine worthy' curves: 'You look amazing,' he whispered, as he nuzzled her in front of the cameras before presenting her with a whole rail of replacement clothes.

'Look how dope this shit is,' Kanye said, and when Kim tried on a low-cut green dress he exclaimed: 'You're getting on best dressed lists now! You're stepping into this territory. You look amazing – it's a new Kim!'

Afterwards Kim tweeted: 'The clothes I got rid of will be up on eBay next month for a charity auction! Going to Life Change Community Church.'

But later it emerged that she had actually been devastated that she could not squeeze into many of the clothes that Kanye had picked out for her. She was said to be 'extremely embarrassed' according to a source quoted in the *New York Daily News*: 'She was busting out of his clothes and even had to go a couple of sizes bigger on some of the dresses. She has been working out like crazy to lose her bountiful booty.'

Kim also admitted that despite the designer clothes at her disposal, she actually prefers wearing comfortable robes, saying she was addicted to the feeling of loose, comfortable robes and that she has to jettison her designer gear and get changed into them immediately when she gets home. Kim prefers light colours for almost all her clothing, and she even prefers to use light towels and bed sheets as opposed murkier colours.

Some of the clothes Kanye had presented her with had been created for his own DW line, a range of designer clothing he debuted at Paris Fashion Week in October 2011, and the rest were bought from European designers.

Kim added fuel to the fire by posting a photo of her behind

squeezed into a pair of extremely tight jeans, writing: 'I think my butt looks too big in these jeans,' and unfortunately many of her followers agreed.

To add to her woes, it appeared at the time that all Kim's efforts to bond with her boyfriend's great mate Beyoncé had proved fruitless. Sources claim the two women barely spoke to each other: 'They were on opposite sides of the stage,' reported the *New York Daily News*. 'Beyoncé didn't even acknowledge Kim was there until the concert was almost over. Kim didn't make any efforts to go speak to Beyoncé either.'

When they both went backstage into the dressing rooms, Kim spent the majority of her time with Kanye and her best friend, PR guru Jonathan Cheban.

'Eventually, the women made small talk in the dressing room, but you could tell Kim was uncomfortable,' added the source. 'She clung onto Kanye the entire time and didn't say much. Kim was talking to Jonathan, and Kanye was talking to Jay-Z and Beyoncé.'

But Kanye continued to be inspired by Kim, and even made reference to her infamous 2007 sex tape in his song 'Clique'. The track, which was leaked to *TMZ*, included the line: 'Eat breakfast at Gucci. My girl a superstar all from a home movie'.

But while he appeared to sing about the sex tape, it was claimed by a source speaking to *TMZ* that Kanye had refused to watch it: 'For all his bad-boy image, he's quite old-fashioned and while they were still just friends he thought it inappropriate to view Kim's tape,' a source revealed. 'Now that they are a couple, there's no way Kanye's ever going to look at it.'

Indeed, he is so sensitive about the tape – which features Kim and Ray J participating in a variety of erotic acts – he has banned anyone in his entourage or circle of friends from talking about it.

The source added: 'When some of his buddies were teasing him about it over a few beers just recently, he went crazy and told them in no uncertain terms that the subject was completely off limits. At first they thought he was joking, but he was deadly serious. Kanye never, ever wants to see the tape'.

Meanwhile Kim was starting to open up about their relationship, publicly declaring Kanye to be her 'perfect match'.

Speaking on American TV show *The View* she said: 'In a perfect world you know when you find someone that you really think is your perfect match.

'I definitely think anything I'd be in now is a permanent relationship,' she added. 'Kids are definitely something I want. I think I wanted that before.'

She went on to explain how difficult she had found ending her marriage to Kris, saying: 'That was really hard on my heart to have to explain to someone something like that.

'I really don't have a lot of regrets. I'm such a different person today. Anyone in my past would probably have wanted the person I am today. I just really have grown up.'

Kim even cheerfully admitted that things were going so well that she had even allowed herself to put on a little weight since they started dating.

'I'm hoping to slim down a little bit, and I'm not afraid to say it,' she told *Life & Style* magazine.

'I think everyone goes up and down in whatever that comfortable love relationship phase is where you like to eat out, but now it's time to get it together again.'

Friends went on to tell how Kim had gained a little weight since the start of the relationship: 'She's gained 15 to 20 pounds. All Kim and Kanye ever do is go out to eat,' a source explained. 'She feels so comfortable around him, he loves her curves, so she hasn't been vigilant about dieting.'

Meanwhile, Kim said that she had once again started taking QuickTrim, the diet supplement she and her sisters were paid to promote. And a few extra curves certainly did not stop her from posing, rather optimistically, in white bridal-style gowns just weeks later. In the accompanying interview for *Tatler* magazine she told how she could not imagine being with anyone apart from Kanye for the rest of her life: 'It's so nice to have a best friend in this game who understands everything you're going through. Being with someone I've known for so many years is comforting.

'He's been there through so many different stages of my life and before I was famous, so this relationship is a different thing entirely. It's good to be aware that he definitely doesn't want anything from me too, because he understands the business.

'I can't even think about being with anyone else than the man I'm with.

'When I look back at interviews I gave [about previous boyfriends] saying, "We're talking about marriage, etc." it's embarrassing. And I really believed it at the time!

'I'm such a hopeless romantic that I'll always believe the next one is the one.'

She went on to explain that if she married again, the wedding would be very different: 'It had always been my dream to have a big wedding, and when people said that I'd made it over the top for the show, that was just me: I am over the top,' she said. 'But the next time, I want to do it on an island with just my friends and family and that's it.'

Meanwhile the couple's open displays of commitment continued. They splashed out on luxury gifts for one another, from Louis Vuitton bracelets to sports cars. And they even began to look for a $10m holiday home in Miami, while Kim was filming in the Florida city.

'K&K have been talking about getting their own place for a couple of months and believe Miami is the perfect location because they both love the city,' a source told *TMZ*. Kanye had been in Paris for Fashion Week, while Kim was in Australia on a promotional tour but when they met up in Miami to film new episodes of her reality TV show, they spent much of their time house hunting.

As well as lavish gifts from Paris, Kanye also brought his stylist, Renelou Padora, to continue Kim's makeover, amid discussions that the couple were planning a joint fashion range to 'seal their relationship'.

'They've both got massive fan bases who will buy their gear,' a source told *The Sun*. 'It's a sign they're in for the long haul and they think it's a romantic way to seal their relationship.'

And according to the source, they both felt that the 'timing is right' for the new business venture. At the time Kim was already designing a fashion line for US department store Sears with sisters Khloe and Kourtney, while Kanye had launched his

DW by Kanye West line a year earlier. The Grammy-winning artist had been told by at least two fashion editors to stick to his day job but was quick to hit back at critics by taking to Twitter to outline his former design work experience: 'I moved to Rome after I left Japan and worked at Fendi for 4 months under cover…I was there to give ideas for the men's collection,' he tweeted.

'I snuck to the Giuseppe Zanotti Factory while still under [my Louis Vuitton] contract and learned to design women's shoes for 2 years before my first show in Paris,' he added. 'I was also offered a position at Versace which I could not take due to my contract with LV which was for 2 years.'

He then went on to explain how he had moved to Paris to open an 'embarrassingly small' design studio: 'Everything I knew about my woman's clothing was what my Mom would wear. I guess some critics would joke that I still don't know anything LOL,' he wrote.

But not everything was perfect in their world. Supposedly, Kim was shocked to learn that her ex-boyfriend Reggie Bush was expecting a baby with his new girlfriend, dancer Lilit Avagyan.

Kim had reportedly been startled by an announcement made by Reggie, who plays for the Miami Dolphins, saying: 'I have a little one on the way. We're pretty excited… It's an opportunity to bring in new life and raise a child.'

Not for the first time, the situation brought huge media attention onto Kim, but she has always handled it calmly: 'I have a love-hate relationship with the paparazzi,' she once said. 'I always try to be gracious. There's a fine line, though, of maintaining your privacy. It's hard when dating and trying to keep things private.

'Sometimes paparazzi show up when you least expect it, though. So I do like to look at least a little bit cute when I go out. And have sunglasses.'

Kim seemed to bounce back from the setback in her usual style, and jetted off to Rome, Venice and Florence to celebrate her thirty-second birthday with Kanye, amid rumours that he was set to propose at any moment. Although her divorce was not yet finalised, a source close to the couple told *Radar* that Kanye had been deliberating over a ring: 'It's only a matter of time before Kanye pops the question,' the insider said. 'They are madly in love with one another and as far as Kanye is concerned, he wants to spend the rest of his life with Kim.

'It's just a case of making sure the ring is perfect because she's his princess.'

Days later, however, the pair were in London for Kim to promote her, Khloe and Kourtney's new fashion range, The Kardashian Kollection, for British high street store Dorothy Perkins, and while there was no ring on her finger, she did sing her boyfriend's praises, saying: 'He's great at boosting my confidence. He gives me compliments in every way possible.'

The couple caused chaos throughout their trip to London, where the garments sold out within hours. Hundreds of fans were camped outside The Dorchester hotel, where they occupied the most expensive suites, and during a series of interviews Kim confessed that her style hero was Kate Middleton: 'She is super-chic and stylish,' gushed Kim, who added that she hoped to have lunch with the Duchess of Cambridge.

Although the lunch date never materialised, Kim received another honour weeks later when Kanye took her to visit his late mother's grave, after eight months together. They were spotted visiting Donda West's graveside in Oklahoma, and after the vigil the couple visited other family members in the area.

A source told *Radar Online* that 'Kanye brought Kim to Oklahoma City the day after Thanksgiving to pay respects to his mother and to meet his mother's side of the family,' a source revealed. 'This was her first time meeting them.' Kanye's mother had died on 10 November 2007 of complications resulting from cosmetic surgery at the age of fifty-eight.

'This was a really monumental moment for Kanye because he adored his mother,' added another source. 'He wouldn't have brought Kim there unless he was completely in love with her.'

And Kim tried to use Kanye's show of commitment to stay positive while her divorce stalled in court yet again. In November her lawyer told a judge that she desperately wanted to move on with her life but felt 'handcuffed' to her estranged husband because the case was still not ready for trial.

Superior Court Judge Stephen Moloney told attorneys for Kim and Kris Humphries to return to court in three months' time, to set a trial date to either dissolve or annul the couple's 72-day marriage.

He did not set a deadline for depositions and other pre-trial investigation to be completed, but indicated a trial could be held early in 2013. Kris was seeking an annulment based on fraud, but his attorney said he needed more time to collect documents from companies that handle Kim's reality shows.

Kim wanted a traditional divorce and her attorney, Laura Wasser, used both the marriage's short duration and a prenuptial agreement as reasons why it should be quickly resolved.

'I don't think his client has a fraud case,' Wasser said in court of Humphries' attorney. 'I think there's a fishing expedition going on here.'

Meanwhile Humphries' attorney Marshall Waller said he needed to be sure he had documents from *E! Entertainment* and NBC Universal before deciding the scope of his case: 'I do understand the desire to get this case moved,' Waller said. 'There's nothing in particular about this case that makes it more important than anybody else.'

Wasser, however, argued that their divorce was not like other cases, saying: 'Ms Kardashian is now handcuffed to Mr Humphries.'

Kim had filed for divorce more than a year earlier, citing irreconcilable differences just weeks after the couple's star-studded and televised wedding. Kris later filed for an annulment.

Wasser said both Kim's mother, Kris Jenner, and Kanye had been deposed in the case, and while neither side showed any side of backing down, it also emerged that Humphries was 'adamant' that he wanted Kim to return the $2million engagement ring he gave her – but she had refused.

Sources claimed that under the terms of their prenup, Kim

would get to keep the 20.5 carat diamond Lorraine Schwartz ring, fair and square. While the former couple's lawyers locked horns in court, both Kris and Kim were embroiled in controversies of their own.

Kris was caught up in an on-court bust-up with Celtics guard Rajon Rondo during the Nets 95–83 win at Boston's TD Garden. And as for Kim, her three-day trip to the Middle East sparked a backlash from some locals in the deeply conservative nations of Kuwait and Bahrain. She did not receive the warm welcome she was expecting due to controversies surrounding her sex tape, short-lived marriage, and a recent furore over her tweets supporting the people of Israel during the conflict with Palestine.

'Her values clash with our traditions as a religiously committed people,' Mohammad Al Tabtabai, a Kuwaiti preacher, told the *Gulf News*. 'Her visit could help spread vice among our youth.'

In neighbouring Bahrain conservative lawmakers also blasted the reality TV star and tried to keep her out of the island nation, calling her 'an actress with an extremely bad reputation'. However, the attempt fizzled out after they could not get the support they needed from their peers and the proposal did not even get to the voting stage. There was also some anger about the high prices of tickets to see her during her visit to Manama, Bahrain's capital.

Tickets to see Kim in person cost as much as 500 Bahraini dinar (over £800), which was more than many Bahrainis earn in a month. And it seemed to Kim that she would never be able to put that sex tape in her past as to add to her misery,

Nick Cannon decided to suddenly say that he dumped Kim after she had 'lied' to him about the existence of the sex tape. Despite calling the reality star 'one of the nicest people you'll ever meet' Nick said that he could not forgive her for denying the tape existed.

Radio presenter Nick, now married to Mariah Carey, briefly dated Kim from September 2006 to January 2007. Speaking on *The Howard Stern Show* he claimed: 'This was my issue. We talked about this tape. And she told me there was no tape.

'If she might have been honest with me I might have tried to hold her down and be like "That was before me" because she is a great girl. She's actually one of the nicest people you'll ever meet.'

But since their break-up Kim has gone on to become one of America's biggest stars, and Nick admitted: 'I think she's a great businesswoman if you ask me.'

CHAPTER 6

A BABY ON
THE WAY!

Kim and Kanye were finally able to silence all the critics and those who doubted their relationship was genuine when they announced they were expecting their first child at the end of 2012. As the happy news spread around the world, the couple received thousands of messages of congratulations.

Kourtney was among the first to express her delight, writing on Twitter: 'Been wanting to shout from the rooftops with joy and now I can! Another angel to welcome to our family. Overwhelmed with excitement!'

Naturally the Kardashians had been dying to share the news, and Khloe added: 'Keeping secrets is hard with so many family members! Especially when you are so freaking excited!!!!! LOVE is everything!!!!' Her husband Lamar Odom posted: 'I'm excited for Kanye and my sister! There's nothing like bringing life into this world! Let's keep God's blessings coming!'

And Kris Jenner, who was already a grandmother to Kourtney's two children, Mason and Penelope, was equally thrilled: 'I'm a happy girl !!!!!!!!! Wowza! Oh BABY BABY BABY!!'

True to form, the pregnancy had been announced in a rather unconventional fashion, when Kanye halted proceedings midway through his performance on stage during a concert in Atlantic City, where Kim was in the audience.

The rapper said: 'Stop the music!' He then announced with a big smile: 'Make noise for my baby mama right here.'

Kim said she felt 'blessed' but admitted her excitement about the baby was tinged with sadness because her late father Robert and Kanye's mother Donda were no longer alive to share in their joy.

On her blog, Kim wrote a message entitled 'New Year, New Beginnings'.

She wrote: 'It's true!! Kanye and I are expecting a baby. We feel so blessed and lucky and wish that in addition to both of our families, his mom and my dad could be here to celebrate this special time with us. Looking forward to great new beginnings in 2013 and to starting a family.'

Kim and Kanye had admitted in the past that their mutual loss of a parent was something they formed a close bond over as their friendship blossomed into romance.

But Kim was unable to relax and enjoy the early stages of pregnancy as a trial date was finally set for her divorce hearing, with a judge confirming a date in mid-June to fit in with Kris's basketball commitments – just weeks before she was due to give birth.

A source close to the situation explained: 'Unless Kim gives in to Kris's demand that she admit the marriage fraudulent, the divorce proceedings will still be on-going and she will still be legally married to him when she gives birth.'

Kris continued to argue that he and Kim married under false pretences, but the source told *Radar Online*: 'Kris isn't trying to drag this out, but he wants to be vindicated in court. Kris will see this through to the end.

'But Kim is refusing to cave to any of Kris's demands. She has moved on with her life, and she won't agree to an annulment on grounds that the marriage was fraudulent .'

Kim admitted that her pregnancy was 'not fun' and told *E! News* that she was suffering from 'growing pains', adding: 'I take lots of naps. Actually I feel really good. This New Year is just about being happy and healthy and that's what I plan on doing.

'I wouldn't say that pregnancy has been easy but there's been no morning sickness. When people say pregnancy is fun and they love it, I would disagree. I think from this stage on it does become easier and funner [sic] but it's just adjusting.

'Even my sister has made it look so easy and it's not as easy as people think. It's a little painful, there's a lot of growing pains. But I've heard it's all worth it so I'm looking forward to that.'

And as for any weird cravings, she admitted a longing for seafood – although it is not encouraged for pregnant women due to potentially high mercury levels: 'I'm craving sushi,' she said. 'But I know I can't really have it, so I'm eating a lot of carrots and celery with lots of ranch dressing.' She also revealed that she had not found out the sex of the baby yet, explaining: 'No preference, I just want a healthy baby.'

But it did not take long for the backlash to start, with Kim facing abuse for hosting a New Year's Eve party at 10ak Nightclub in Las Vegas in the early stages of her pregnancy, reportedly earning herself $300,000. After she posted a photo of herself and fellow reality TV star Brittny Gastineau, she faced barrage of hateful comments. Many Twitter and Instagram users made cruel remarks about her weight, with one labelling her, 'no fit mother' while another called her 'fat', adding 'lose some weight'.

She was also described as being 'busted and old news' and even drew criticism for tweeting about her new scent, Pure Honey, when really she should have been focusing on motherhood.

The criticism then went to spark a further backlash, with fans and anti-trolling campaigners reacting angrily, leaving their own messages of support and describing the 'haters' as 'losers' and 'lowlifes'.

Margaret Morrissey of campaign group ParentsOutloud said: 'My New Year Wish would be that people could be stopped writing on social networking in this way.

'Miss Kardashian is not the only one who suffers from this abuse, and it is abuse, it needs to be made illegal. Why do people think they can be abusive and rude online mostly to someone they do not know and have never met?

'It is hurtful and is not necessary and needs to be followed up by the police as remarks on Twitter are. We need to set our young people examples and some decency rules to live by. Being famous does not mean people can target you with nasty rude remarks.'

In fact Kim was the latest in a line of celebrities with babies to have been targeted by internet trolls. Just three months earlier the singer Adele had been targeted after the birth of her baby boy was announced. Within minutes shocking tweets threatening to kill both Adele and her son had been posted. Other cases have involved *X Factor* judge Gary Barlow, who was taunted after his daughter was stillborn.

But regardless of the criticism, Kim and Kanye decided that they would allow their baby, and their adjustment to parenthood, to appear on reality TV. *E! Entertainment* network president Suzanne Kolb told the *Hollywood Reporter*: 'Kim and Kanye are an incredibly dynamic couple, and their baby news is just so exciting. Like so many Kardashian fans, we love it when this close-knit family gets even bigger.

'We look forward to sharing the joy as they prepare for more diapers, more bottles and without a doubt, more fabulous baby wear.'

And Kim's mother and manager Kris was said to be thrilled about the possibilities the baby would bring, including a new show. A source told *HollywoodLife.com*: 'Probably the most excited person is Kris. She let us all know that this will be the theme for a new reality show, the best Kardashian show ever.

'They are going to document everything about Kim's pregnancy, but I don't know how Kanye feels about that.'

An astute businesswoman like Kim, who had put her name

to everything from fake tan to fragrances, saw no reason to wait for her baby's birth to promote her new celebrity trainer, Tracy Anderson. 'Tracy Anderson is keeping me in shape!' she wrote after working out with the fitness guru, who has famously trained A-list stars including Madonna and Gwyneth Paltrow.

'She is helping me make the adjustments necessary to keep me feeling happy, healthy and most importantly, create a workout plan that is safe for the baby.

'It's really important for me to have a fitness routine that works for my body and my schedule and I'm really happy with the workout plan Tracy is working with me on.'

Meanwhile Anderson added: 'Because she's Kim Kardashian, I am able to pay more attention to her workout, so I check in with her all the time, and she is doing amazing.

'She doesn't love to do the dance part, but she's a really smart girl and she knows that you're going to get out what you put in.

'She's got, like, a very iconic sexy body, she's not somebody that I would want to take her amazing curves and turn it into something emaciated.

'She's such a hot girl so it's like, let's keep that body like that!'

While it is not known whether Kim received payment for the write-up, Tracy coincidentally was promoting a series of nine exercise DVDs for pregnant women, entitled *The Pregnancy Project*. Having Kim onside was sure to do wonders for sales, since her endorsement is known to hold plenty of influence with her millions of fans. And Anderson's new workout playlist, created with rara.com, features some of Kanye's tracks.

But Tracy is known for her outspoken views too. She sparked controversy when she told *DuJour* magazine: 'A lot of women use pregnancy as an excuse to let their bodies go, and that's the worst thing.'

Tracy, who was a new mother herself at the time, had struggled to lose weight following her first pregnancy. She explained her remarks later on *Good Morning America*, saying: 'Pregnancy is difficult and every pregnancy is completely unique. We crave a lot. I think in today's society where we have all of this pressure to look a certain way, I feel like they turn to diet a lot because that's what works for them because fitness routines usually let them down.

'So when they do get pregnant it's like, "Oh my gosh!" It's not just like, "I'm going to let my body go for this pregnancy," it's also, "I can eat all the things that I never let myself eat."

'I see people that come to me after pregnancy and they didn't need to necessarily gain that much weight.'

Meanwhile, Kim turned down a substantial offer to document the remaining months of her pregnancy on a specialist pregnancy website. David Dginguerian, an Armenian filmmaker, wanted to launch a membership-only website called *MyPregnancy.com*, with Kim as its gestating poster girl. In a pitch letter to Kim, Dginguerian suggested such a site could 'generate $100,000 a month,' with the money going to the 'Christian Charity' of Kim's choice. And as a sweetener, she herself was offered $250,000 as a 'signing bonus'.

She and Kanye were also said to have turned down a huge

$3million offer for the first exclusive photos of their yet-to-be-born child. A source told website *TMZ* _that the couple had been 'flooded' with lucrative offers from media outlets desperate to be the first to publish the baby pictures.

Similarly, Brad Pitt and Angelina Jolie were offered a $4.1million payout following the birth of their first child, Shiloh, in 2006, although that was dwarfed by the $14million they received after the birth of their twins, Knox and Vivienne, two years later. The couple donated the payments to a charitable trust they had set up.

Many were surprised at Kim's decision to turn the money down, but it was thought that Kanye was behind the move as he was becoming increasingly uncomfortable with the way she had been putting every aspect of their life under constant public scrutiny. And of course with their combined fortunes the pair had no financial need to accept the cash.

Instead they put their efforts into renovating their first home together, ensuring everything was perfect for the baby's arrival at their $11million Bel Air mansion.

The luxurious home, in a private gated community in the exclusive California suburb, was already a whopping 10,000 square feet before the couple decided to add an extra 4,000 feet to complete their Italian-style villa, with wrought iron staircases, a gym, movie theatre, hair and make-up salon, bowling alley, basketball court, indoor and outdoor pool. Not forgetting a nursery, of course. There is also an extensive library, massage room, stunning infinity pool, complete with pool house, and a large grassy lawn with spectacular hillside views.

Needless to say, the pair were thrilled to be joining a host of A-list neighbours including Jennifer Aniston, Los Angeles Clippers basketball player Chris Paul, and founder of the *Girls Gone Wild* entertainment franchise, Joe Francis.

To buy the mansion, Kim sold her 4,000 square foot Beverly Hills' home to a buyer who wanted all her furniture too. For just under $5million, the price included every piece of furnishing, including couches, mirrors, coffee tables and even the rugs. Kim had wanted a quick sale and did not bat an eyelash at seeing her top-quality furniture, even her beloved custom-built vanity dresser, go – all of it worth hundreds of thousands of dollars.

She originally bought the Mediterranean home in 2010 for $4.8million, so although she made a loss on the sale of the five-bedroom villa, Kim was delighted to move on to the sprawling property she and Kanye had bought to start their family together in style.

Designed by architect Ron Firestone, the listing for their new home said: 'Custom craftsmanship and old world details are combined with every modern amenity.

'Hand forged wrought iron and glass front doors open up to the two-storey formal entry with black walnut parquet floors. A two-storey living room flanked by Cantera stone columns overlooks the rear grounds and mountains beyond. The great room includes wide planked floors, beamed ceilings and a stone fireplace and features a bar and stone wine cellar.

'The library serves as a warm respite, detailed in rich woods and a burgundy marble fireplace.

'The master suite has spectacular views from every window,

a fireplace, sitting room, large walk-in closet and changing area. The master bathroom has a large steam shower, spa tub and massage room, while the massive backyard is a dream with sweeping lawns, an infinity edged pool and a loggia that serves as an outdoor living room and kitchen.'

And it was no surprise that the baby was expected to be the most pampered tot in Tinseltown when it arrived.

With multi-millionaire reality TV and music royalty for parents, a source told *Grazia* magazine that Kim and Kayne were reportedly looking to spend '$100,000' (£62,500) on a nursery, and that Kim had bought the same $8,000 (£5,000) baby furniture from Petit Trésor as the Duchess of Cambridge. While in the UK promoting the Kardashian Kollection for high street store Dorothy Perkins Kim had been inspired by the Duchess.

Kim said at the time: 'We hope to bump into Kate and William while we're over here. She's is so stunning and he is such a class act.'

Kim confirmed that her baby, just like Prince George, would also be very much in the public eye, but admitted that her unplanned pregnancy was 'a miracle' as she had secretly battled fertility issues: 'It's kind of a miracle that I even got pregnant,' she told host Kathie Lee Gifford on *The Today Show*. 'Khloe has been very open about her fertility issues and I think I was always really kind of quiet about mine, and I have similar issues.'

Kim's younger sister Khloe has openly talked about her distress following her failure to conceive during three years of marriage, with initial tests revealing she was not ovulating.

Kim explained: 'It was a pleasant surprise when so many doctors were telling me one thing and then the opposite happens.'

Before her pregnancy Kim had revealed how shocked she was to learn she had fertility problems: 'When I went to the doctor a couple of months ago, he took tests to check my hormones and my levels, and everything was really suppressed and really low because I've been on birth control for so many years.

'I want to have kids one day, so he really suggested that I get off birth control. I'm thirty-one, and my egg levels came back as a woman that's in my 50s. I'm concerned just hearing all this information of how every woman is born with a certain amount of eggs, and that number can never be increased.

'Maybe this just isn't on the cards for me, and I'm freaking out a little bit. It's so overwhelming, it's even made me second-guess even wanting to have kids. Whatever's meant to be will be. If I'm not supposed to have kids then maybe I don't want kids.'

A source suggested to *Radar*: 'Yes, her oestrogen levels were low, but she had been on the pill for a very, very long time.'

The insider also added that she had not suffered the same fertility issues as Khloe: 'Kim's doctor assured her that once she had been off the pill for a few months she shouldn't have any issues conceiving,' the source said.

But once the news of her pregnancy had been officially announced to the public, Kim said she found it hard to believe she was really going to be a mother: She said in an interview on *The Today Show*: 'I think until I really start seeing, like, a belly, it won't really sink in. It's just like a weird realisation until you really start seeing the physical changes, and every day's different.'

In the same frank interview, she also went on to discuss the possibility of a third marriage, to Kanye: 'It's something that we talk about, but I think it's just, right now, focusing on the baby,' she said. 'I'm so content with how things are right now. And how life is and we're so happy. We definitely want that in the future, but I'm not in a rush.

'What I've learned in life is, I was always such a planner, and you think your life is going to be a certain way, and the best surprises just happen when you don't plan.'

She also revealed that she had been surprised by Kanye's very public announcement of her pregnancy, while he was on stage: 'Once you're past the three-month mark, you're pretty safe, so he just kind of goes off with what he feels and he was feeling it that night,' she explained.

As always with Kim and Kanye's rollercoaster life, however, another setback was just around the corner. Just as they were throwing themselves into preparing for parenthood, an ex-girlfriend of Kanye's decided to issue an excruciating public warning to Kim about her boyfriend's 'obsession with sex'.

Brooke Crittendon dated Kanye for two and a half years after meeting him backstage at a gig in 2004 when she was working as a production assistant for MTV. And while their relationship was all hearts and flowers to begin with, she told how the Grammy-winning musician's 'insecurities' quickly began to get in the way of their happiness, with him once refusing to even go on stage until Brooke reassured him about their relationship.

But the couple eventually called time on their long-term romance because Brooke wasn't comfortable with 'sharing' her man with other women.

She added in an interview with *The Sun* newspaper: 'I was never OK being one of many, or even one of a few. Kanye was very open and honest but it ended up with me knowing too much. I don't want to be silly and say it wasn't cheating because I knew about it.

'He definitely had an appreciation for the feminine form and a curiosity. As a celebrity, sex becomes cheap but his obsession with sex was more sophisticated.'

Although Brooke believes curvy brunette Kim is just his 'type', she has warned that having kids could merely be a matter of 'ticking a box' for Kanye.

She explained: 'In Hollywood, you cannot say "forever". Them being together satisfies them for now. Having a baby ticks a box. She wanted kids and it's his legacy.'

Brooke went on to suggest that Kanye's decision to settle down was influenced by his pal Jay-Z, who had a baby daughter Blue Ivy with superstar wife Beyoncé.

On top of all that, it was alleged that at the end of January, Kris Humphries turned down a huge offer to settle their divorce case, which looked set to rumble on throughout Kim's pregnancy. According to *RadarOnline.com*, Kris, who was asking for an annulment on the basis of fraud, refused to accept the monetary payment in order to bring their lengthy divorce battle to an end.

A source close to proceedings told the website: 'After Kim filed for divorce, she offered Kris a payoff, with the agreement that he would not continue to pursue an annulment to their marriage.'

However, Kris is said to have turned down the offer because it had 'never been about money'.

The source added: 'He wants to be able to marry in a church again, with a clear conscience, when he finds someone special. Kris is deeply religious and he believes that the only way he can do that is if his marriage to Kim is annulled.'

Meanwhile a spokesperson for Kim denied that she made the offer, however, and contrasting reports suggested that she was in fact refusing to pay Kris anything, and she even demanded that he should cover the legal costs of the case. It was estimated that both Kim and Kris had spent in the region of $250,000 each so far on the as-yet-unfinalised bitter feud.

Kris then claimed that the divorce was being unnecessarily rushed because of Kim's pregnancy. The basketball star's lawyer, Marshall Waller, filed new documents accusing Kim of trying to use the situation to speed up a settlement. Waller stated that Kris had nothing to do with her 'unplanned pregnancy' and it should have no impact on their litigation.

The documents also stated Kris's desire for further delay in the trial because key witnesses had yet to be deposed and he had not received various documents he said he needed. He wanted raw footage of episodes of the Kardashian reality shows and records from Ryan Seacrest Productions, E! Entertainment Productions, and Bunim-Murray Productions to illustrate how he was badly portrayed in the shows, but no footage had been turned over.

The documents stated: 'Indeed, if as Ms. Wasser asserts there really is "no evidentiary support" to support Humphries' claims, why don't they just give us the access we want? What are they hiding? What is there in the raw footage of this televised courtship, 72-day marriage and resultant breakup that they are so afraid of us discovering?'

Meanwhile Kim's lawyer, Laura Wasser, argued that her client's estranged husband 'cannot continue to hold the Court and Kardashian hostage through his own lack of diligence in preparing his case for trial'.

Wasser was said to be furious that the divorce trial was delayed because of Kris's NBA basketball schedule, and was seen comforting Kim as they went into a meeting together, hand in hand.

Wasser has a reputation for being the go-to legal eagle for many of Hollywood's biggest stars. Her past celebrity clients have included Heidi Klum, Ryan Reynolds, Angelina Jolie, Christina Aguilera, Mariah Carey, Stevie Wonder, Kiefer Sutherland, Nick Lachey, Kelis, and Britney Spears.

And on the advice of her hotshot lawyer, Kim filed a legal declaration in which she said the pressure of the case was standing in the way of her happiness and also threatened 'the health and well-being of my unborn child'.

She said she wanted a divorce as quickly as possible because: 'It will help create a new, full life for me, and the same should hold true for [Kris].'

Kim also said that Kanye was eager to sign a Voluntary

Declaration of Paternity when their child was born, but he would not be able to if she was still married.

Kim's mother Kris said in a TV interview the same week that her daughter was under great stress due to the divorce dragging on so long: 'Kim has been going through this divorce,' said Jenner. 'She has been under a lot stress because of it.

'She had a bad week. The doctors told her the stress is going to be a problem with pregnancy.'

There were further delays and setbacks when Humphries' lawyer, Marshall Waller, suddenly quit, blaming an 'irremediable breakdown of the attorney-client relationship'.

And Kim began to fear that the drawn-out divorce could have 'long-term effects' on her baby when she had to be treated for severe abdominal pains. In February 2013, Kim's doctor rushed to her home in the middle of the night to examine her and warned her to reduce her stress levels, and her mother confirmed she had been told to relax.

'Kim has been going through this divorce for months,' Kris explained. 'She has been under a lot of stress because of it and the doctors told her she had a really tough week and the stress could become a problem if she isn't careful.'

But in a revealing interview with *DuJour* magazine just weeks later, Kim said she was having an easy pregnancy, with no morning sickness, no cravings and no fatigue.

'I used to always say I can't wait to get pregnant because I will just eat whatever I want, but it's completely different,' she told the magazine. 'I'm like, OK, I want to eat as healthy as possible.'

In fact since she rarely drinks alcohol, Kim admitted that

her biggest challenge had been cutting back on her favourite drink, Diet Coke, which she replaced with the occasional iced tea.

But she was not too concerned about the occasional unhealthy treat: 'Lately I've been watching shows like *I'm Pregnant And Addicted To Meth*. It definitely makes me feel better if I'm wanting one sip of Diet Coke or, you know, too much sugar. I'm like, "This woman is on meth."'

Having already signed up with superstar trainer Tracy Anderson in a bid to make losing her baby weight that little bit easier, she went on in the same interview to talk about her figure, saying she still preferred clinging clothes as they make her look more petite: 'I think because I have big boobs it could make me look heavier if I don't, like, show off my waist or something, so I just have kind of learned to dress one way only.

'Khloe can wear flowy, pretty things because she's really tall. Kourtney is, like, really little. I'm just kind of in between, so it doesn't really work.'

She went on to talk about her relationship with Kanye, saying he had 'taught her a lot' about privacy: 'I'm ready to be a little less open about some things, like my relationships. I'm realising everyone doesn't need to know everything. I'm shifting my priorities.

'When you live your life so publicly, like on a reality show, people assume that they know every side of you already. But they always want more. Doing a TV show with your family, it's really hard to hide or be guarded.'

After the couple revealed amid great excitement that

their baby was to be a girl, Kanye took Kim to visit his grandfather, Portwood Williams Sr, in Oklahoma City, where she reportedly impressed the ninety-seven-year-old with her beauty, manners and riches, and afterwards he said he thought she was a 'sweet' girl.

Growing up, Kanye's grandfather was one of his biggest influences, taking a great interest in his grandson's career and giving him advice. But he warned the rapper that marriage rarely lasts, adding that he would not attend if he married Kim, although his own marriage to Kanye's grandmother Lucille had lasted an incredible 72 years.

According to *The Sun*, when Portwood was told that Kim's previous marriage had lasted just 72 days he laughed, saying: 'They didn't make it. But I want everybody to be happy and evidently she got who she wanted now. She's found a good man.'

Kim took an interview opportunity to explain that she simply had not been ready for marriage before she met Kanye: 'Sometimes you're just not ready,' she admitted to *Cosmopolitan*. 'A person could have it all, and you're not ready for it all.

'But this is where I probably always should have been. Marriage is something I know that we both want in our future, but I don't have this sense of urgency about it.

'I have this best friend who understands me and helps me through all my tough experiences, and vice versa, you know? It just feels like this is it for me. I've always said that I wanted kids, but I don't think I ever would have been ready until now.'

But she admitted that it also took her some time to realise

that having a child does not necessarily have to be done in the traditional way, and she had been judgmental when her eldest sister Kourtney fell pregnant in 2009: 'I was like, "You're not married! How could you do this?" I was really firm and strict. But she was like, "Marriage isn't what I want." And later, I realised she had a better family life than I did,' said Kim.

And while she too would not be married before the baby was born, Kim said she would not rush into marriage again, as her sister Khloe had done – she married Lamar Odom within a month of meeting him: 'I saw fast marriages like Khloe and Lamar's and that was what seemed to work. Now I say give it a good six months before you commit. Feelings change, even if it seems so lustful.

'I used to think, Well, can you really have it all? The truth, the excitement, and the passion? Now I know you can.'

But with motherhood now firmly on the horizon, Kim planned to cut back her schedule into more manageable chunks, only picking work she loved doing.

She added: '2013 for me is about scaling back. I want to focus on the few projects that I'm super passionate about and not spread myself too thin.'

Kim was exhausted, but as always she did not wish to appear ungrateful or complaining: 'I yawn a lot. All the time,' she said. 'When I'm at a shoot and everyone breaks for lunch, I'll just go and have half a nap. I can sleep anywhere and even a few minutes rejuvenates me.

'One weekend I had several events in Las Vegas. So the night before I left I had a spray tan at midnight, went to bed at one, and then left early in the morning. I got to my hotel and right away went into hair and make-up for three hours. I ordered room service so I could eat at the same time.

'I went to the first event, came back, changed really quickly and had to head down to a dinner. I got full before the main course, and it was already 11.30 – and I still had another event to go to after dinner. So I excused myself from the table. I went back up to my room and took a nap while everyone else was eating their main course. I set an alarm for fifteen minutes, napped, went back down, met everyone, and headed to another event at a nightclub.

'Everyone just thought I had gone to the bathroom.

'The ability to power nap is so valuable. I wish I could tell you how to do it but I'm afraid you either have it or you don't. I do need a dark room or an eye mask on, but then I just close my eyes and I'm out. Some lucky people like me can do it, but not everyone can.'

Despite her promises to keep out of the spotlight for a while, Kim could not resist an intimate photo shoot for a glossy French magazine called *L'Officiel Hommes*. In the atmospheric black-and-white photographs Kanye was snapped holding his girlfriend's left breast as she gazed at the camera. Clenching his fist with his right hand, the rapper planted his lips firmly on her face as she expertly smouldered in the highly stylised images by influential photographer Nick Knight.

The cover showed an apparently naked Kanye embracing Kim, and another raunchy shot inside the magazine showed Kim covering his eyes with one hand, and pulling open his mouth with the other. However, the shoot was seen by many as being somewhat out of character for Kanye, who had been notoriously private about his life aside from music and fashion. And some critics feared he had been persuaded to do it by Kim who, it emerged, was earning up to $100,000 for each of her personal appearances at the time.

One day after announcing that she was expecting she had been paid $153,000 for her appearance at a Las Vegas nightclub. Three weeks later, the expectant mother supposedly earned an incredible $200,000 for attending a private party in Cote d'Ivoire, Africa. Briefly attending an event in Nigeria four days later was apparently worth a whopping $500,000. And just for turning up at the Topshop opening in West Hollywood she earnt herself $50,000.

She was fast becoming one of the most powerful celebrities in the world, being paid $25,000 per tweet as a sponsored Twitter user, endorsing products that included bathing suits, candles and even Charmin toilet paper.

On top of that, she had supposedly received a huge settlement from Vivid over her infamous sex tape with rapper Ray J. Money was also pouring in from sales of her three perfumes, a line of watches, their Khroma Beauty lines, an at-home laser removal product and the Kardashian Kollection for Sears, producing between $200million and $300million in sales in 2012, with the family due a hefty cut of the proceeds.

The family also signed a $40million contract extension to make a further three seasons of *Keeping Up With The Kardashians* but it was not as if they needed the money, since they were said to have been left a $100million estate in trust by Robert Kardashian when he died, almost a decade earlier.

Kris's marriage to Bruce Jenner helped boost the family

coffers as the former decathlete was reportedly worth a further $100million on his own.

But Kanye confessed he feared his fans might be deserting him as a result of his relationship with Kim. He was unhappy when MTV's *Hip-Hop Brain Trust* voted him the seventh Hottest MC in the Game, and said his ranking would have been higher were it based solely on his music skills.

Speaking to US radio station Hot 97's DJ Enuff, he said: 'Yeah, number seven bothers me. To me, I feel like in order for them to put me as number seven, they had to bring up things they didn't like.

'I don't know, it's definitely not based on a body of work. It possibly could just be like overall rap-MC-swag. What happens is, with these types of things, they don't like "Givenchy Kanye", they don't like Kanye in a kilt, they don't like Kanye in a relationship.'

But Kanye had bigger things to worry about when just days later, in March 2013, Kim was rushed to the doctors, amid fears she had suffered a miscarriage. She felt ill shortly after arriving back in Los Angeles from Paris and made an emergency trip to the physician.

A source told the *New York Post*: 'Kim started feeling ill on the plane from Paris, and called friends as soon as she landed. She was rushed to her doctor in tears. She thought she was having a miscarriage.'

Kim was discharged at around 12.30am the following day, after the doctor had reassured her that both she and her baby were fine.

Sister Khloe let all of Kim's fans know that she was okay,

posting on her blog: 'A lot of you have expressed concern in the recent hours about Kim, and I just wanted to let you all know that mommy and baby are doing fine and just taking it easy right now. Thank you so much to all of our wonderful fans and loved ones for your concern and support. We love you!'

However, Kim's physician is said to have told her to slow down, and exercise less. Alongside trainer Tracy Anderson, Kim had been working out seven days a week in a bid to keep her pregnancy weight gain under control.

Previously Kim had said that while she had been working out to maintain her daily exercise regime, she knew she would pile on the pounds during her pregnancy although she had been doing her best to eat healthily. She told American TV show *Extra*: 'I have the biggest sweet tooth and I love junk food,' she admitted. 'Being pregnant I don't like any of it. I'm waiting for the moments when someone's like, "Let's go to McDonald's and Taco Bell" – that's not happening for me and I'm kind of sad about it.

'I want to have those cravings, like cheeseburgers, but I haven't. Now I eat healthy I don't know what's going on,' she added.

Despite the scare, and her promises to scale back, Kim's schedule continued as frantically as ever, with her jetting down to Atlanta for the premiere of her movie, *Tyler Perry's Temptation: Confessions of a Marriage Counselor*, in which she played Ava, the protagonist's bitchy colleague. But her performance was so harshly criticised she was named Worst Supporting Actress at the Razzies in March 2014. One critic labelled her performance as 'vapid, nasal and awful'. And while she looked radiant at the premiere, she revealed on the red carpet that she had not been finding her pregnancy as easy as she had hoped: Being pregnant is not as easy as my sister [Kourtney] made it look or as my mom has made it look,' she told *E! News*. 'It's a little painful at times. I've gotten sick a couple of times and that puts you out, especially when you travel. It's getting a little more difficult.

'I'm craving carrots and ranch dressing,' she added. 'I used to love sweets, I used to love chocolate, can't even eat chocolate!'

While she seemed determined to keep her pregnancy weight under control, Kim's aunt, Joan Kardashian, let slip that she was considering surgery to snap back into shape: 'She can have a tummy tuck, which will take care of most of her weight fears,' Joan told *Now Magazine*. 'Other than her belly, which is rather flat, every other part of her body has ballooned. And this is Kim holding to a strict diet. Imagine if she let herself go?'

'The family's trying to convince Kim to relax and worry about losing the weight months from now,' she added.

It seemed to be impossible for Kim to avoid stress, however, as she was called to a nine-hour secret divorce deposition at her lawyer's office Insisting she did not marry Kris Humphries to boost ratings for her reality show, Kim maintained she really did love the sportsman when he popped the question.

Lee Hutton, the new lawyer representing Kris throughout the divorce proceedings, was probing for evidence to prove that Kim had married the sports star to boost ratings and consequently 'defrauded' him.

While Kris was hoping for an annulment – rather than a divorce – sources told *TMZ* the lengthy deposition 'didn't help his case'. He did not turn up for the hearing, and Hutton is said to have 'not asked much at all about the reality show and whether it was staged', despite previously threatening to 'blow the lid off' the alleged fraud. But Kim refused to submit to Kris's demands, instead insisting she married for love, however misguided she may have been at the time.

She was hoping to obtain her divorce before the baby was due, and was of course concerned about the effects the drawn-out divorce could have on her unborn child, according to her mother, who said: 'Kim has been going through this divorce for months.

'She has been under a lot of stress because of it and the doctors told her she had a really tough week and the stress could become a problem if she isn't careful.'

To add to her stress, Kim felt under fire for her maternity wardrobe choices, which were routinely analysed by magazines and fashion experts. She said on her show *Keeping Up With The Kardashians*: 'It's part of my job to look chic at all times,' she explained. 'And as if Kanye has the time to dress me every day. I feel bad that Kanye gets the bad rap for dressing me, it's so rude.

'I don't want to give my boyfriend this bad rep because for some reason everyone blames him for dressing me. I feel so much anxiety. He couldn't care less what people think, he said he'd love me no matter what I wear.'

And she admitted that she was getting worried about

choosing the perfect name for their unborn child, hinting she would like to keep up the family tradition of choosing a name beginning with K.

She said: 'I think it would be really cute because Kanye and I are both Ks, but half the names on our list aren't Ks. We still have time, whatever feels right. Kanye, being the father, wants something that's unique. We have a list, and some of them are K names, some of them aren't.

'North is not on our list,' she claimed. 'But you know what name I do like – but it probably won't be on our list. I like Easton – Easton West – I think that's cute.

'I think it's really cute now that my belly has popped a little bit. I think it's really a sexy thing,' she added. 'It's just such an exciting thing for the guys to see our body go through all these different changes. Kanye loves it and embraces it and he's helped me feel sexy and embrace it.'

In the same interview she went on to say that she had been feeling hormonal and upset by criticism of her changing body shape 'I think it's a little bully-ish to call a pregnant woman fat,' she said. 'I mean, what do you expect? I hope I gain weight. I'm a little heavy.

'I think it's kind of mean just all the comments that I see, whether it's, "She's wearing heels!" That makes me feel good and sexy at least being heavier so if that makes me feel good, my baby will feel good,' she explained.

'My momager [how the family sometimes refer to mum Kris] will not be handling anything for the baby because the baby is hopefully not going to do anything to be in the business or have a show, or do anything like that,' she said, adding that she would still support her child, should she choose to pursue a high-profile career.

Kim herself has always loved being in the public eye, and makes time for her fans. She explained in *Kardashian Konfidential* that whilst some celebrities go to club events and never leave the VIP area, she has always preferred to get out amongst the crowd and mingle, snap pictures and get into the spirit of the night. She recalled a night in Las Vegas – just after the launch of her fashion range – seeing five girls wearing full outfits from the line and waving to them to come over. She has always tried to remain approachable rather than join in with the aloof manner that some celebrities adopt.

She added that although being filmed during childbirth was a 'beautiful experience' for her sister Kourtney, she herself would not have cameras documenting the intimate moment: 'I don't even think I'll have a camcorder,' she said. 'I don't even know if I would want that as a memory.'

But bad memories continued to haunt Kim, as her ex, Ray J, decided in April 2013 to release a new single called 'I Hit It First' about his notorious relationship with her. The cover featured a blurred-out picture of Kim, and the lyrics clearly referenced his sex tape with her that catapulted her to stardom after its release in 2007.

And in an interview with hip-hop radio station Power 106, Ray J spoke about Kim and Kanye, saying: 'Life is a rollercoaster, so you never know what's gonna happen. But I wish 'em the best, much success to both of 'em.

'Yo, this whole thing is like a Magic Mountain experience.'

Kim chose to ignore the controversy, and instead diverted

attention by announcing that she had planned to freeze her eggs to boost her chances of conceiving in later life, had she not got pregnant naturally with Kanye.

She told her sister on their reality show Keeping Up With The Kardashians: 'I just cannot believe I am having a baby. Kanye and I are like, "Is this happening?" Oh my God! Am I ready for this? Like, can I handle this?

'The whole plan with my doctor was to go to Miami, get off birth control, really clean out my system, freeze my eggs and I got pregnant. I was freezing my eggs because I did not want to get pregnant right this minute, I wanted to wait until I got divorced and hopefully remarried.

'This whole experience for me has been just shocking, exciting, but shocking.'

She also admitted that she was 'nervous' about breaking her happy news to younger sister Khloe as she and husband Lamar Odom had struggled to conceive.

By April 2013, although Kanye was being sued for allegedly sampling a tiny portion of an obscure song without obtaining the rights for his international hit 'Gold Digger', the couple finally received the news they had been waiting for. Kris settled their divorce after 536 days of bitter negotiations, leaving Kim and Kanye free to start planning their wedding, and Kim could have her baby without still being married to Kris.

Although the divorce battle had lasted five times as long as the marriage itself, Kris eventually backed down. He was perhaps forced to consider mounting legal costs, which were no doubt a hefty consideration. Once Kris dropped his pleas for an annulment, the judge signed off divorce papers and dissolved the marriage.

But Kris, who was ordered by the judge to attend the hearing so he could face fines for his previous failure to show up in court, skipped the appointment.

It had been a bitter battle, with each camp going back and forth with claims of betrayal and deceit. A source even claimed that Kim had arranged for photographers to snap them on their honeymoon trip to Italy's Amalfi Coast: 'Kris was the one to push for the honeymoon. Kim didn't want to go on the honeymoon because they were scheduled to move to New York City to begin filming *Kourtney & Kim Take New York*,' a source told *Radar Online*.

'Kim finally relented. Kris was absolutely dumbfounded when a photographer appeared out of nowhere and started taking pics of them by the pool. Kim happily posed.'

Kim attended the final legal hearing alone, and barely raised a smile when a judge granted her divorce: 'I think this is a reasonable way to resolve this case,' said Superior Court Judge Hank Goldberg, who did not disclose terms of the three-page settlement agreement.

But sister Khloe revealed that the stress of the drawn-out divorce had taken its toll on Kim's health during her pregnancy: 'Her back hurts, her breasts hurt, her stomach hurts, her feet hurts, her head hurts, her eyes hurt, her nails hurt. She cries all the time, too,' said Khloe.

But in the same interview with TV host Ryan Seacrest, Kim herself tried to put a more positive spin on the situation: 'I do think I would get married again,' she said. 'That's what I've always wanted. And just because you think you find it and you realise that's not it, I think I was brave enough to realise that quickly and not waste time. I found what I really wanted. So I think I definitely do want that.

'Kanye loves watching the show. He travels so much that it's just not a reality for him to be there, and be on but he loves to watch it. He loves the whole experience.

'I've changed a little bit on showing relationships,' she added. 'I felt like I gave so much of myself publicly. And when you make mistakes it's embarrassing. I'm going to be a mum, so I feel myself getting really protective.'

And she was not the only one feeling protective – soon after that interview, Kim scored a longed for invitation to Anna Wintour's glitzy Met Ball, where Kanye sang to his girlfriend in front of an A-list crowd, telling Kim to ignore the haters.

Kanye was seen serenading the mother of his unborn child with: 'Let nobody bring you down, you're so awesome.'

And it seemed that Kim wanted to reciprocate the love, tweeting a picture of Kanye to her Instagram page, along with the caption: 'Baby you're AWESOME'. The couple had arrived on the red carpet at the fashion event together, with Kim showing off her baby bump in a custom-made Givenchy dress by Riccardo Tisci, unable to keep the smile off her face at finally being included in one of the most exclusive events of the year.

However, fashion critics slated Kim for her floral maternity gown, and even comedian Robin Williams weighed in, saying that he wore the look better as a cross-dressing octogenarian nanny in the movie *Mrs. Doubtfire*.

Kim said afterwards: 'For me, having people criticise what I wore and looked like when I was pregnant, that was hard. It made me feel insecure, so I have tried to avoid the limelight more.'

Clearly happier than ever, she set about planning a lavish baby shower. Invitations in the style of children's musical boxes were sent out for the party in June, with each white box playing a lullaby version of Kanye's track 'Hey Mama' as a plastic ballerina – which bore an uncanny resemblance to Kim – danced.

The family chose a 'garden chic' theme for the bash at the multi-million dollar Beverly Hills home of Shelli Azoff, wife of West's former manager, Irving Azoff, and Kris Jenner's best friend.

Khloe revealed that Kanye broke with tradition and put in a brief appearance at the televised shower, along with Kim's brother Rob, Khloe's husband Lamar and Kourtney's boyfriend, Scott Disick: 'It's girls, but Kanye will come at the end,' said Khloe. 'I said I want Rob to be there the whole time because I feel bad he's, like, left out of all this stuff.'

And Kim took the opportunity to gush about how excited she was to be expecting a daughter: 'I am so excited to be having a girl, who doesn't want a girl? I know that's really what Kanye has always wanted. He wanted a little girl.'

She also hinted that her unborn child might follow in her father's footsteps and be a musician: 'I feel like my kid is going to need musical things. What kind of child will I have? A very tutu-y, like, princess? I just can't wait to see what she's going to talk like and look like. I am so excited about the joy she is going to bring into our lives.' Onlookers were surprised that there were no celebrities invited to the shower, and despite their new-found friendship, Beyonce did not attend the party either.

But as usual Kim's excitement was tinged with anxiety as she was forced to respond to a shocking report that claimed she was risking her baby's health by having Botox injections during the pregnancy.

Under fire from all sides, Kim admitted how vulnerable she felt about the future, writing on her blog: 'As I'm counting the days until I finally get to be a mother, I'm a bit nervous and anxious, but also excited, knowing that I learned from the very best.

'My mom is a strong and ambitious career woman that despite her busy schedule and the millions of things she has going on, she still manages to put family first and continues to look out for us everyday.

'Motherhood is a gift and I know after watching my mom do it, it's not easy, especially when trying to balance a career. I can't wait to follow in her footsteps and make her proud like I am of her.'

Kim added that Kourtney – who has two children of her own, Mason and Penelope – had also been a strong mentor: 'She is super woman with her ability to effortlessly balance work with taking care of two amazing kids and I am so lucky to have her as my guide and confidante as I too become a mother.

'I love being an aunt. It's definitely showed me how hard moms work. When I babysit, I realise it's a lot harder than I thought.

'It's funny because Kourtney didn't seem like someone who wanted to be a mom. She never babysat Kendall and Kylie. Whenever she talked to kids she wasn't all warm and fuzzy, like she wouldn't ever talk baby talk. She'd say, "No way! I'm not changing my voice for anyone!"

'It was so cool to see Kourtney warm up after she had Mason. She changed into a completely different person.'

But while she was happy to bare her soul, Kim went on to admit in an interview with *Fabulous* magazine that she was worried about protecting the privacy of her unborn child.

'I'm definitely more of a recluse since I was pregnant,' she admitted. 'But I haven't necessarily decided to hold myself back, it's just preparing myself for respecting the privacy of my child and my boyfriend.

'We live different lives, but I love being open. That's who I've always been. That will never change because that is who I am.'

She added, however, that she took comfort in the fact that her little sisters Kendall and Kylie Jenner had grown up so well, despite spending most of their lives in the glare of the limelight.

She also complained about living life in the spotlight, with a surprising Twitter rant about the paparazzi and wanting to have a break from the constant scrutiny: 'I get I live a public life,' she wrote. 'I live my life on a reality show for the world to see. I love my life, but when the cameras stop, that doesn't mean I don't want a break too.

'I'm 32 yrs old now, about to be a mom. I'm not 25, clubbing around LA anymore.'

But just two days later she sent a very public message to Kanye, sharing a photo collage of her favourite magical moments, which she created in honour of his thirty-sixth birthday.

'Happy Birthday to my best friend, the love of my life, my soul!!!! I love you beyond words!' she tweeted, along with the sentimental collection of six photos that Kim chose to express her devotion – including moments captured both in their public life, and private glimpses of them enjoying one-on-one time. In one shot the pair were seen snuggling up closely together in a sweet self-portrait, while in another they raised glasses over a romantic dinner.

But while Kim continued to cope with the scores of photographers trying to catch a glimpse of her, Kanye did not seem to be enjoying the experience of becoming tabloid fodder so much. He appeared to be increasingly distancing himself from the Kardashian clan despite becoming a part of their family.

When the couple first started dating Kanye appeared to embrace their fame and what went with it, even agreeing to appear on *Keeping Up With The Kardashians* to show his support for his girlfriend. But with a baby on the way it seemed he could not handle the constant attention and admitted that he would not be returning to the show because of the 'backlash' his last appearance had generated: 'You know, the amount of backlash I got from it is when I decided not to be on the show anymore. And it's not that I have an issue with the show, I just have an issue with the amount of backlash that I get.

'Because I just see, like, an amazing person that I'm in love with and want to help,' he told *The New York Times*.

He went on to say that he said he felt it was his duty to protect Kim and their child: 'This is my baby, this isn't America's baby,' he added when asked his thoughts about parenthood: 'One of the things was to be protective, that I would do anything to protect my child or my child's mother. As simple as that. I just don't want to talk to America about my family.'

In the same interview he took the extraordinary step of comparing himself to genius Apple boss, the late Steve Jobs.

Less than a week away from the launch of his much-hyped new album, *Yeezus*, Kanye did not hold back in the far-reaching interview: 'I don't have one regret,' he went on. 'If anyone's reading this waiting for some type of full-on, flat apology for anything, they should just stop reading right now.'

Among his forthright comments, he said in reply to a question about his cultural relevance: 'I think what Kanye West is going to mean is something similar to what Steve Jobs means. I am undoubtedly, you know, Steve of Internet, downtown, fashion, culture. Period.'

And when asked about the future, Kanye replied: 'I will be the leader of a company that ends up being worth billions of dollars, because I got the answers. I understand culture. I am the nucleus.'

But his remarks were widely mocked and condemned, with the *New York Post* calling them 'dumb', *Entertainment Weekly* said the interview was a 'study in the art of narcissism' and *Us Weekly* described his quotes as 'obnoxious', adding: 'One flaw Kanye West clearly doesn't have is low self-esteem.'

The controversial interview came in the same week as Canadian glamour model Leyla Ghobadi falsely claimed in *Star* magazine that Kanye had cheated on Kim – claims Leyla would later swiftly backtrack on.

But at the time, Kim's representatives flatly denied the outlandish claim, while Kanye's added: 'This most recent attack on Kanye West and his family is totally without merit. It's a blatant attempt by a misguided individual who is clearly seeking publicity, and another in a series of malicious stories drummed up by non-credible "news" sources.

'This is a sad attempt to hurt two people trying to live their lives.'

In the hope of escaping the scrutiny, Kanye flew off to Switzerland for a surprise performance at Art Basel, a modern art exhibition. But during his trip, he also spoke of the difficulty of dating a reality TV star, saying he had to constantly battle the public's perception of him: 'I fight in my position of being a very commercial celebrity boyfriend. I fight to push culture forward every chance I get.'

He could not stay away long, however, as Kim was rushed to see her doctor again with a suspected case of appendicitis. Suffering severe stomach pains, she was filmed sitting on an exam table with a thermometer under her tongue as the medic delivered the worrying news that she could have appendicitis. 'That got me anxious because of your blood count,' he told her. 'This could be appendicitis. We really don't want to operate on a pregnant woman because it has potential complications for the pregnancy. If we really feel strongly that this could be appendicitis, then sometimes we have to operate.'

But Kim simply replied: 'Getting appendicitis while pregnant is not fun. It's not easy, it's going to be really tough to go through.'

CHAPTER 7

THE ARRIVAL OF NORTH WEST

The final few weeks of her pregnancy were agony for Kim, who went into labour five weeks ahead of her scheduled delivery date. Kanye cancelled an appearance at a release party in Los Angeles for his new album *Yeezus* to be present for the birth of their child in a private birthing suite at Cedars-Sinai Medical Center – the hospital of choice among many celebrities, including Britney Spears, Victoria Beckham and Jessica Simpson.

Before the birth Kim had discovered she needed to go into emergency labour because she was suffering from pre-eclampsia, a condition that affects some women towards the end of their pregnancy, caused by high blood pressure or hypertension, and can lead to serious complications for the baby. After some panicky calls to her sisters the family rushed to the hospital – where Kim addressed her unborn child on a camera phone.

In footage that was released later, she said: 'Okay, so we are officially going through with this, I am so excited to meet you. Your dad is on a plane and he literally lands now. He's going to freak when he realises he's going to meet you really soon.'

Moments before baby North was born, weighing in at 4lb 5 oz, Kim added: 'I am freaking out!'

According to sources, the singer stayed by Kim's side throughout the entire terrifying ordeal: 'Of course, Kanye was there with Kim when she went to the hospital and had the baby,' *Us Weekly* reported, adding that: 'He wouldn't have missed the arrival of the couple's bundle of joy for anything.'

Kim had planned to have a C-section but after suffering an infection and being warned by doctors that she was most likely suffering from the life-threatening condition pre-eclampsia, she was forced to deal with giving birth weeks before she had expected in order to save the life of her baby girl.

With her 'blood pressure skyrocketing' and 'the baby in distress' according to *Us Weekly*, she had no choice but to grit her teeth and get on with a natural delivery, with Kanye by her side throughout every moment of the terrifying ordeal.

The baby was born on 15 June 2013 although Kim's due date had been 12 July – just one day after the Duchess of Cambridge gave birth – and what would have been Kanye's mother Donda West's sixty-fourth birthday. But given the early birthday, the littlest Kardashian was placed in an incubator, while Kim struggled to get to grips with breastfeeding: 'Kim is doing it but seems like she's having trouble,' reported *Radar Online*. 'She is planning to keep trying to do it for a little while longer but she may end up switching to a bottle.'

Kourtney had been a driving force behind Kim's decision to feed the baby naturally, according to *Life & Style* magazine: 'Kim wasn't going to, but Kourtney is a huge proponent of breastfeeding. Kourtney also told Kim how much breastfeeding helped her lose the baby weight.'

Kim's friend Robin Antin, with whom she had spent the last few days of her pregnancy relaxing in the sunshine, revealed how Kim's bravery had impressed Kanye: 'This was a lot to go through,' the founder of music group GRL explained. 'I'm sure she was exhausted but she handled it like a pro. Kim was scared but Kanye was more nervous. He asked a lot of questions as he paced about, they were both quite quiet.'

He went on to tell *Us Weekly*: 'When I walked in to see her, Kim was holding the baby. I said: "Oh my God, you're a natural." Kim said: "I know – it's so weird."'

In the aftermath of the birth, doctors warned Kim that she would need to watch her blood pressure, as hypertension could be a real issue after an emergency procedure of this kind.

'After discharge she should follow up with blood pressure checks,' a source told *Us Weekly*. 'The condition can cause problems after birth. For the next two weeks, Kim wants Kanye around 24/7,' the mole continued, adding that the couple would also employ the services of a nurse for a year.

'Kim is a bit freaked out, but the baby's breathing is fine,' the magazine reported.

Within hours of the birth congratulations were pouring in from all over the world. And Beyoncé Knowles put to rest any suggestion that she and Kim did not get along by writing on her blog: 'Congratulations Kim & Kanye, enjoy this beautiful moment together – Beyoncé.'

And while Kim's hospital room was filled with flowers, she insisted well-wishers were not allowed to bring any tasty treats for her to eat as she was focusing on getting back into shape. Kanye was back to business too, writing four new songs about his daughter in the days following her birth.

Before they could make an announcement about the child's name, however, her birth certificate was leaked, revealing they had named her North West – 'Nori' for short. Editor-in-chief of *US Vogue* Anna Wintour was said to have given the baby's name her personal seal of approval.

The inspiration behind the film *The Devil Wears Prada*, Wintour apparently raved about the suggestion when the couple dined at her New York home on the eve of the Met Gala in May 2013.

'That's not why they named her North, but it's nice to have Anna's blessing,' reported *E! News*.

There had been widespread speculation that Kim would follow her family's 'K' tradition but she admitted months before the birth that her baby name list was varied: 'Some of them are K names and some of them are not,' she had told chat show host Jay Leno, back in March.

In the same interview Kim laughed at the comedian when he brought up rumours Kanye wanted to name the baby North. Kim had apparently preferred the name Kaidence, and she liked the idea of calling the baby 'Kai' for short.

Kim's close friend Larsa Pippen was one of the first to visit the baby in hospital. Larsa told *E! News* 'We kind of went back and forth and the name that I wanted, Kim didn't love,' she said, adding that Kanye had barely left Kim's side since the birth: 'He's so cute, he doesn't leave the room. He's, like, in love with the baby. It's so cute.

'She's doing great. She's feeling really good and excited and the baby is so freaking cute.'

It was revealed on Piers Morgan's CNN talk show that only a handful of people had met the already famous offspring, but among them was Apple co-founder, and all-around super-geek, Steve Wozniak.

Wozniak appeared on *Piers Morgan Live* and gave his account of what led to the bizarre meeting of the minds: 'I have seen a lot of babies, and a baby represents the love between the people and that meant more to me and the love that Kim was showing to Kanye.

'Just because he was interested in technology and companies, she, as a birthday present, she had me come up there to meet him,' he explained.

After leaving hospital in the middle of the night to avoid photographers camped outside, the family moved into Kris Jenner's six-bedroom property in Hidden Hills, and Kim's mum spoke of her joy at becoming a grandmother again: 'I love the name North. I'm pro North, absolutely,' she said. 'The way Kim explained it to me was that North means highest power, and she says that North is their highest point together and I thought that was really sweet.

'It's North West, but you don't walk around calling some-body, "Hi North West," it's just North.'

There were also reports that Kanye had taken to fatherhood

too, changing nappies and learning how to swaddle the baby, although there were moments of heartache as he continued to mourn the loss of his mother: 'It's made him miss his mom very much,' an insider revealed. 'He wishes she could see his beautiful baby girl.'

As expected, the entire Kardashian clan rallied around Kim and her baby. Kendall and Kylie were living at home anyway, but Kourtney and Khloe were daily visitors to their niece.

Kris and Bruce, who chose to be known to their latest grandchild as Lovey and Grandpa, tactfully relocated to their Malibu beach house to give the new family some privacy.

Kris revealed in *People* magazine: 'They call me Lovey and Bruce is Grandpa. At first I was Grandma, and all of a sudden I didn't like the way that sounded. My mom had a friend called Lovey and I thought that was the cutest name.'

She added that Kanye was a 'spectacular dad' and explained how she had insisted they move into her house as soon as the baby was born: 'You don't want to be all the way on the other side and you need one of us,' Kris said she had told her heavily pregnant daughter: 'You're going to be isolated in Beverly Hills with a baby.

'Live with me in this gorgeous house. That would be the perfect scenario.'

Within weeks of giving birth, Kim took to her blog to write: 'These past couple of weeks have been filled with the most exciting experiences of my life. I'm enjoying this time to fully embrace motherhood and spend time at home with my family.

'I've been reading all of your messages and want to thank you all for your sweet thoughts and best wishes. It truly means everything to me. I am so blessed to have the support of my family and fans in this beautiful moment.'

And Kanye could not resist breaking his own self-imposed privacy policy either to share details of the unique present Kim gave him for Father's Day. He tweeted a photograph of two Apple computer mice signed by the company's founders, Steve Jobs and Steve Wozniak.

And before long he was back at work, talking about his new family at a concert in Connecticut. He told the crowd he was still mourning his mother, and wished she could have met her granddaughter. During a heart-felt speech he said: 'These past ten years have been amazing.

'There's been some ups and downs. I made some mistakes and I've made some accomplishments. There's only one thing I regret, there's only one thing I wish I could change out of everything that's ever happened.

'I wish that my mother could've met my daughter.'

Kanye continued to talk about the effects her untimely death had had on him during an appearance on Kris Jenner's chat show. He said: 'There were times [after her death], I would put my life at risk. I didn't have something to live for. Now I have two very special people to live for, a whole family to live for, a whole world to live for.'

But as his hugely successful 'Yeezus' Tour drew to a close, meaning he would have more time to spend with Kim and Nori, the couple were faced with yet more unneeded controversy.

A new story hurtfully claimed he was canoodling with another woman while Kim was at home with their newborn. But it was swiftly proved to be untrue when the blonde magazine founder who was accused by *Life & Style* magazine of getting 'cosy' with Kanye West at a BET Awards after-party later came forward to deny the report. In fact Viva Glam's Katarina Van Derham said Kanye would not even have had any idea who she was, despite the fact their paths briefly crossed at the event.

She told *Radar*: 'Poor Kanye. He doesn't even know who I am! I never got introduced to him.

'We never even said a word to each other. They're just looking for stories. I feel bad for him.'

And far from being on the hunt for ladies, she said the macho Kanye seemed far keener on having fun with the actor Jamie Foxx and some other male friends. She said: 'I didn't even see him talking to other girls!'

But perhaps the sleepless nights with the baby were getting to Kanye, as he was charged for attacking a photographer who fired questions at him at Los Angeles International Airport as he made his way home from the tour.

He was then told he might face a felony attempted robbery charge stemming from the airport altercation during which he charged at a paparazzo, who was unfortunately the same man attacked by Britney Spears wielding an umbrella in 2007. The victim was taken to a hospital following the incident and told the authorities that he wanted to press charges against Kanye.

Police officers referred the case to the Los Angeles County District Attorney's Office as a felony attempted robbery rather than the lesser charge of battery, since the cops suspected that Kanye had committed an attempted robbery when he struck the photographer and tried to take his camera.

Above left: Style evolution: a soulful Kanye rocks a vintage Christmas jumper as he gets ready to take to the mic in New York City, March 2004. The jumper hasn't been seen since.   © *Dimitrios Kambouris/Getty Images*

Above right: Kanye – with another retro jumper - and the Drop-Out Bear backstage at MTV's Total Request Live show in 2004.   © *Theo Wargo/WireImage*

Below: Kanye takes a hit and keeps the Playboy Bunnies entertained during a break at the 2006 Superbowl.   © *Marc Andrew Deley/FilmMagic*

Left: Khloe, Kim, Ne-Yo and Serena Williams party round a giant burger at McDonald's Big Mac 40th Birthday in Malubi, 2008.

© Chris Polk/FilmMagic

Right: …but Kim clearly managed not to take a nibble herself, as she shows off an unbelievable figure in Miami Beach weeks later.

© John Parra/WireImage

Left: Kim looks stunning as she leads then-husband Kris Humphries through the Amber Fashion Show in Monaco, 2011. © Mark Thompson/Getty Images

Above: The Kardashian clan – Kim, Kourney, Khloe and Kris – strutting it at the Kardashian Khaos store opening in Las Vegas.　　　© *Ethan Miller/Getty Images*

Below: Signs of things to come: Kanye can't keep his eyes off future wife as they pose with Kourtney at a glitzy Hollywood Christmas bash.

© *Michael Bezjian/WireImage*

Above: Battle of the booties: Kim and ultra-curvy rapper Nicki Minaj pose down for the cameras at the 2012 BET Awards. © *Johnny Nunez/WireImage*

Below left: Outlandish: Kim styles a mermaid outfit for a Halloween party in New York. © *Josiah Kamau/FilmMagic*

Below right: And the masters of disguise are at it again days later in Miami!

© *John Parra/WireImage*

Kim and Kanye at Cannes Film Festival, for the première of Kanye's critically acclaimed short film 'Cruel Summer'.

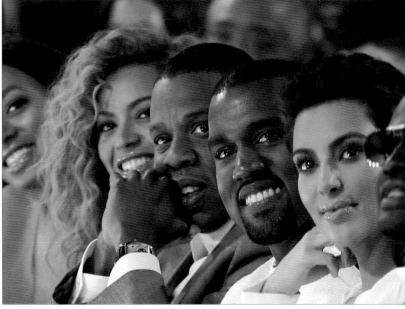

Above: Kanye rocks the mic in a spectacular performance in Atlantic City, New Jersey.
© *Kevin Mazur/WireImage*

Below: Beyonce, Jay-Z, Kanye and Kim make up a star-studded front row at the 2012 BET Awards.
© *Chris Polk/Getty Images*

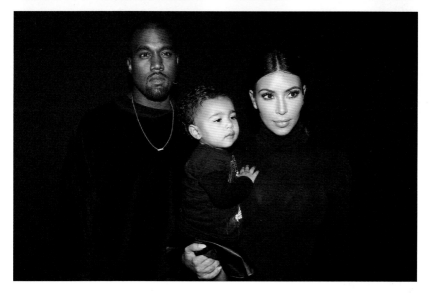

Above left: A heavily pregnant Kim wears a striking floral dress on the red carpet in NYC. May 2013.
© *Jamie McCarthy/Getty Images*

Above right: Mum and daughter: Kim smiles at a very cute 13-month-old North West.
© *GVK/Bauer-Griffin/GC Images*

Below: The family smoulder in matching black at the Paris Fashion Week in September 2014.
© *Betrand Rindoff Petroff/Getty Images*

Kim and Kanye:
the world's
ultimate celebrity
couple.
© Dimitrios Kambouris/
Getty Images

Kanye was surrounded by about five paparazzo who captured the incident as he left with his bodyguard in their car, and it was eventually decided that he would not be prosecuted, as there was no reason to suspect he was trying to steal the camera.

Perhaps as a result of his run-in with the press, Kanye insisted on turning down a lucrative seven-figure magazine offer for the first photos of North, deciding instead to follow the lead of close pals Jay-Z and Beyoncé in releasing the first picture themselves.

Jo Piazza, author of *Celebrity, Inc: How Famous People Make Money*, suggested in her book that Kanye hated the idea of 'pimping' his child, despite his own reputation for massive self-publicising.

During a special interview with Kim's mother, taped when North was just two months old, Kanye proudly gave fans the moment they had been waiting for – their first proper look at the baby.

When the snap flashed up on the screen it was clear from the image that the tiny baby possessed features from both her mother and father.

'How cute is that gorgeous baby!! Who do you think she looks like?' Kris gushed over the photo, to which Kanye responded with a laugh: 'I pray that she looks like her mother when she's older.'

Kris told the singer: 'I think she is an amazing combination of the two of you. She is so adorable. She has Kim's eyes, I think she has your cheeks and both of your lips. Some days she has your lips and some days she has Kim's lips.

'They dissect her,' Kris explained to the audience. 'Kim would go, "Look at her ears, Mom, look at her ears!" It is so cute how obsessed you guys are.'

Before revealing the picture, Kanye categorically denied that he and Kim had tried to shop first images of their daughter to the media. He spoke on Kris Jenner's chat show, saying 'It's all this talk about baby pictures and can you get paid for the baby picture or do you want to put it on a magazine?' he explained. 'And for me and your daughter we have not attempted to get paid for anything, we have not attempted to put it on a magazine.

'You just stop all of the noise and I thought it would be really cool on her grandmother's season finale to bring a picture of North,' he said.

During the emotionally charged interview he told Kris: 'Now I have two really special people to live for, a whole family to live for. A whole world to live for.'

He also addressed the criticism he had received for being in a relationship with media-loving Kim: 'I had people say, "This is going to damage your credibility as an artist or a designer." But I say I don't care, I love this woman.

'Or someone could say, "When the paparazzi surrounds you, everyone knows you don't like the paparazzi. Why would you be with this person?" And I say, "I am being with this person because, you know, I love this person and she is worth it to me."'

Kanye added that he was taught by his late grandfather, Portwood Williams Sr, who had died at the age of ninety-eight weeks before the interview, that life is all about having 'joy'.

'My grandfather just passed and his whole thing, it was never about money and it was never about popularity, his whole thing was joy,' said Kanye. 'Just joy. Like having joy in his life. And she's Kim, my joy, and she brought my new joy into this world.

'And there is no paparazzi and no blog comment, there is nothing that is going to take that joy away from me.'

Kanye also admitted that before he and Kim got together, he would dream about the reality star. But he told Kris that he would not be behaving as Tom Cruise famously did during an interview with Oprah Winfrey, by jumping up and down on her couch in 2005.

'I just dreamed about being next to her. I keep saying it. I don't want to start jumping up and down on the couch or anything,' said Kanye, to which Kris replied: 'Oh please! That would be so fabulous!'

Kanye joked that he had been so keen to date Kim that he considered switching careers because she had been out with a stream of sports stars before him. He also admitted that he would draw himself in next to Kim on the Kardashian family Christmas card.

Even after revealing the photo, the couple were still plagued by photographers desperate for another glimpse of the baby. And they found themselves under even more intense scrutiny than ever after the US President Barack Obama bemoaned the 'change in culture' and referenced *Keeping Up With The Kardashians* for their opulent lifestyle warping the American Dream.

At the Kindle Single interview the President talked about

his own childhood, saying: 'There was not that window into the lifestyles of the rich and famous.

'Kids weren't monitoring every day what Kim Kardashian was wearing, or where Kanye West was going on vacation, and thinking that somehow that was the mark of success.' Indeed the President had twice referred to Kanye in the past as a 'jackass'.

After the singer upstaged Taylor Swift at the 2009 MTV Video Music Awards, Obama famously called him a 'jackass' in an interview with CNBC, adding that he prefers rapper Jay-Z over Kanye.

He acknowledged liking Kanye and the singer's Chicago roots, explaining: 'He is a jackass. But he's talented.'

But Kris Jenner hit back at Obama for pointing out that Kim and Kanye live in a 10,000 square foot house: She said on her own talk show 'I bet the President has some friends with 10,000 square foot houses and he probably wouldn't mind going over there when asking them to have a party for campaigning for dollars to run for president,' she said. Kris also thought it was strange that Obama was singling out Kim and Kanye: 'I find it so odd that he's picking on Kim Kardashian and Kanye West. Well, Kanye West, first of all, doesn't go on vacation. Ever.

'And Kim Kardashian is the hardest-working young lady in the world. She never sleeps, she never stops, she never slows down and works so hard for what she's got,' she added.

Despite this criticism, the couple decided to take a leaf out of the President's book and upgrade their personal security. Since money was no object when it came to buying high-performance armoured vehicles to protect his family, Kanye was inspired by the President's car, known as 'Limo One'.

Kanye spent over $2million on two Prombron Iron Diamonds by Dartz Motorz, but then was embarrassed when the Latvian company faced a backlash from animal rights campaigners PETA for featuring leather interior made from the foreskins of whale penis.

But Kanye still wanted the SUVs which the makers insisted were 'built to withstand attacks from landmines and rocket-propelled grenades'. And while beefing up security for his family, the rapper also hired two more bodyguards and body doubles that could be used as decoys for the paparazzi to chase.

'If there have been any kidnapping threats already against their daughter, he isn't saying. But that fear is clearly in his mind,' a source told *Daily Star*.

And according to a source in *Us Weekly*: 'Kanye doesn't leave North for more than an hour. He holds the baby all the time.'

Unwilling to be parted from his three-month-old daughter, Kanye convinced Kim to join him on his 23-date North American concert tour. There had been reports that she was unwilling to go along on the tour, with *Radar* suggesting the reality star was more interested in maintaining a regular schedule for herself and baby North: 'Kim is very unhappy that Kanye won't be around as much because of his work,' the website said, adding that the star was 'contractually obliged' to remain in LA over the winter for the filming of her family reality show.

However, a source close to the family told *Radar* that they would stick together: 'Nori will be back at the hotel. The new parents don't want her to be exposed to a lot of people, and random strangers.

'Kim thinks she and the baby will remain with Kanye throughout the North American leg, but life on the road is going to get very old, very fast.

'Kim is used to being the centre of attention, even though she has a baby, some things will never change.

'Changing hotels every few days, trying to keep Nori on a sleep schedule will be very hard. The likely scenario is that Kim will join Kanye in major cities such as Los Angeles, Las Vegas, Chicago and New York. Kanye doesn't want to be away from the baby for more than three days.'

Kanye was planning to tour Europe after wrapping up his American leg in Miami, but Kim was thought to be unenthusiastic about accompanying him. The source added: 'If Kanye thinks Kim is going to follow him around the world, he is delusional. She isn't a piece of luggage, or a member of his entourage.

'Kim will happily camp out in Kanye's Parisian apartment, but she certainly won't be waiting in the wings at the end of each of his shows. She has her own life, and it will be very interesting to see how the couple deals with this next phase of their relationship.'

And Kanye showed his respect for Kim's independent lifestyle in an hour-long interview with BBC Radio1, saying it was her immense $40m fortune that makes their relationship so successful. 'She was in a powerful enough situation, where she could love me without asking me for my money, which is really hard for me to find,' he said.

'She gave me everything. She gave me a family. She gave me a support system.'

Kanye added that in a few years' time their baby should be paid every time her image is sold by a photographer: 'You see all these cheques you're getting age six because people are taking your picture, you don't have to worry about a thing ever again just because people want to take your picture, and I made that happen, Nori.'

Anything but bashful, Kanye ended the interview in typical self-aggrandising fashion, saying: 'Rap's the new rock 'n' roll. We the rock stars and I'm the biggest of all them.'

Having kept a low profile since giving birth, Kim then decided to make her comeback in style, posting a raunchy portrait in a skimpy white swimsuit. The picture immediately sent shockwaves around the world, with the *MailOnline* website receiving a staggering 3,163 comments within hours, many readers feeling that it was 'inappropriate behaviour' from a new mother.

One Twitter user wrote: 'Kim Kardashian you are a MOTHER now I don't think posting pictures of your ass on Instagram is appropriate'.

Worse still, Kim received messages from users calling her 'nasty', 'disgusting, and looking 'nauseatingly huge'.

There were also complaints of Kim and Kanye being 'obsessed with themselves' and slamming Kim's behaviour as a bad example for their daughter. Comedienne Jenny Johnson, who is known for her dislike of the Kardashians, re-tweeted

Kim's post with the sarcastic comment, 'You're an amazing mom'.

But while Kim's tweet may not have gone down too well with her critics, it certainly had the right effect on Kanye, who re-posted the snap on his Twitter page, with the message: 'HEADING HOME NOW'.

She explained later: I was trying on a bathing suit and I actually just sent that to my boyfriend – my fiancé – and I was like, "Babe, can I post this up? This is my, like, big middle finger to the world on everyone that called me fat."'

Kim had put on 50 pounds while pregnant with North, but she was distraught at being called 'fat', 'obese' and 'Shamu' by various bloggers.

'It really hurt my soul,' she said on the *Tonight Show*. 'It changed how I am in the public a little bit. There were these stories where I was, like, 200 pounds. I was gaining weight because I was pregnant and it was really hard to read all these stories and hear all these nasty things.

'And I think people sometimes question, they think I'm out in hiding now.'

But Kim and her family have always handled public scrutiny calmly: 'We recognised a long time ago that the paparazzi were just trying to do their job. So we're usually nice to them.'

Kim also wrote in her book *Kardashian Konfidential* that she always tries to smile when she sees photographers in the hope they will get the picture they want, and go away. And she admitted that she tries not to let the online abuse bother her.

On the problem of media-generated paranoia, she admitted that at first the sisters would read all the bizarre rumours people said about them and even get upset at each other for reading out the most hurtful online quotes. But they quickly learned that a little communication goes a long way and when they scratched the surface it would always emerge that the quote had been taken out of all context.

Their attitude now to people questioning their talent to success ratio is just to say it's okay if people doubt their talent so long as they can see the sisters have put in the work to get to where they are and be successful. You can't win around everyone, so they try to focus on being happy with their own success.

In fact, Kim even said that in the past, people who were completely set against the Kardashian clan finally met them and found themselves won over!

The now-famous white swimsuit picture showed off the amazing results of Kim's new weight loss, helped by the Atkins Diet.

'I've actually been doing the Atkins Diet and love it,' she confessed.

A spokesperson for Atkins confirmed: 'She is eating lots of lean proteins, healthy fats like nuts and avocado, carbs, fruits, veggies and cheese. She wanted to be a healthy, nursing mom and not toxify her milk with her diet, or lose weight too quickly. She's been doing Atkins since her doctor approved it at the end of June.'

Although she appeared happy with her weight, Kim still felt compelled to answer back to allegations that she had implants to make her buttocks appear larger.

She furiously wrote: 'I'm seeing all these nonsense tabloids claiming I have butt implants-injections. Get a life! Using pics of me 15lbs skinnier (before I had my baby) comparing to me now!

'I still have weight to lose. Anyone who has had a baby knows how hard it is to lose weight (especially the last bit of weight) & your body totally changes! Making fun of me pregnant & making fun of me trying to lose weight now shame on you.

'I'm not perfect but I will never conform to your skinny standards sorry! Not me. And BTW I've lost a lot so far & I'm proud of that! Don't give young girls a complex!'

However, Kim revealed that she was delighted with even the most intimate areas of her post-baby body – just days after giving birth she confessed she had been examining her vagina in the mirror and considering a naked *Playboy* shoot.

'When I came back from the hospital the first thing I did was go and look at my vagina in the mirror. It looks better looking than before,' she told her sister Khloe while filming an episode of *Keeping Up With The Kardashians*.

'I just want to come out to the world, and be naked and be like, "I look so hot. I am back," she added. "You called me a whale, Shamu, a cow."'

Running the risk of irritating many new mothers, Kim then brushed off childbirth, saying: 'Labour was honestly the easiest thing ever. I did not feel one thing. Like, it was not hard.' And she went on to say how deeply and quickly she had bonded with her daughter: 'And then just staring at her, everything that they say that happens is so true, like you fall so in love and it's this deep connection. I just want to spend time with her, with Kanye.

'Literally we just watch movies, we just chill. I get so much work done, like thinking of ideas of stuff that I want to do.

'Becoming a parent is everything you could ever imagine and more. It's the best feeling and it's the most rewarding job. I recommend everyone go through the process.

'Kanye doesn't want us doing baby pictures, with Kanye it's a different dynamic. I'm still an open book and I still share my life but I guess you can't expect everyone else to want to jump into a career that they just don't want to be in,' she said.

And the moment she was back in shape, Kim seized the opportunity to revamp her style to please Kanye, admitting she always dresses with her rapper beau in mind because she wants him to think she looks 'really hot'. She even said she would be prepared to ditch an outfit if her man decided it didn't look good.

In an interview with *The Sunday Times Style* supplement, Kim said: 'You want your guy to think you're really hot. I'll put something on and he'll say, "No, that doesn't look good", and I'll trust him.'

Kim also revealed that her style has changed since she and Kanye welcomed little Nori into the world, and admitted she is very decisive when it comes to her daughter's clothing choices.

Asked whether she dresses differently now she's a mother, Kim added: 'I want to dress a little lighter colour-wise. I think North looks cute in light colours, and then I want to wear light colours. North doesn't typically wear pink, though. She wears mauve or blush, not, like, typical baby pink.'

CHAPTER 8

SHE SAID YES!

As baby Nori turned five months old, the question on everybody's lips was when would her parents tie the knot? And the world finally got the answer it had been waiting for on 22 October 2013, when Kanye pulled out all the stops to lay on one of the most lavish proposals in showbiz history.

Never one to do things by halves, he rented out an entire baseball park to pop the question, and true to form sealed the deal with a $1.6 million ring.

As the couple celebrated Kim's thirty-third birthday at the AT&T baseball park in San Francisco, Kanye gave his girlfriend the surprise of her life when suddenly the message 'PLEEEASE MARRY MEEEE!!!' flashed up on the field's scoreboard screen. At that moment Kanye presented Kim with a 15-carat diamond ring by jeweller Lorraine Schwartz and, as he slipped the ring on her finger – and she screamed 'Yes!' – fireworks exploded into the sky.

At the same time a 50-piece orchestra struck up, first playing Lana Del Rey's 'Young and Beautiful', from the film *The Great Gatsby*, followed promptly by Kanye's own hit with Keri Hilson and Ne-Yo, 'Knock Me Down'.

Kim's family and friends then poured out of the dugouts where they had been hiding. Kanye chose the venue because it's where his sporting idol Barry Bonds hit his record-breaking 756th home run. In the past he had professed his admiration for the baseball legend, naming a song after him in 2007.

It later emerged that renting out the space for a private event costs $200,000, with another $20,000 for use of the scoreboard, although *E!* reported the owner of the San Francisco Giants gifted the use to Kanye, who was among the guests.

But money was certainly no object for Kanye, who spent $15,000 flying in 50 handpicked members of the couple's family and their closest friends by private jet, having personally invited them and sworn them to secrecy. They included 'several Silicon Valley billionaires', reported *TMZ*. However, not everyone was there to celebrate the romantic moment, as it was revealed afterwards that Bruce Jenner was 'not invited to AT&T Park and he had no idea his step-daughter was getting engaged', although Kim later explained that he would be walking her down the aisle at the wedding.

The orchestra were paid up to $1,000 apiece as a reward for their discretion; four times their normal rate. And the fireworks display that lit up the night sky had cost upwards of $25,000. Just a couple of days earlier, Kanye had dropped a hint about his big plans, telling the audience at his concert in Seattle that he planned to marry Kim 'one day'.

Within moments of agreeing to marry him, Kim had posted a snap on Instagram, holding her ring finger towards the camera as she flashed her dazzling engagement band while smiling broadly alongside her man, with the simple caption: 'Yes!!!'

Afterwards she revealed: 'I was shaking so much, shaking the entire time! Like, "Is this really happening?" It was like an out-of-body experience.'

But Kim wasn't the only one caught off-guard by the *Yeezus* rapper's proposal. Although he had asked Kris Jenner's permission before he went ahead, the rest of the family were also none the wiser, convinced they were merely attending Kim's birthday celebrations.

Kim added: 'Everyone there thought it was a surprise birthday party. Everyone – my sisters – it was such a surprise.'

Kanye had actually been in Los Angeles earlier the same day, attending the Hollywood Film Awards, where he presented director Steve McQueen with a special honour, so Kim was unsure whether he would be able to celebrate her birthday with her at all. But Kanye had taken care of every detail, and oversaw the entire creative process of making the ring, and when it came to choosing someone to collaborate with he knew exactly who to turn to – Kim's favourite jewellery designer and close friend, Lorraine Schwartz.

'Kanye was involved in every single way. He had a vision from the beginning. He looked at a lot of stones and he wanted only the best,' a spokesman for Lorraine Schwartz told *E! Online*.

'He and Lorraine emailed back and forth, and stayed up nights discussing how he wanted it to be. He wanted the diamond to look like it was floating on air. Everything was his idea from beginning to end.' The spokesman added that the stone was, of course, completely perfect.

'The ring is flawless. Not just internally flawless, it's flawless. It's a D-stone, the best diamond there is, type 2A. It's a perfect cushion-cut diamond.'

Schwartz is a favourite among the A-list, having previously created gorgeous bling for many other celebrities, including unique engagement rings for Blake Lively and Beyoncé Knowles. But she was also behind Kim's previous engagement ring from Kris Humphries, designing the huge 20-carat diamond ring he used to propose to the reality star two years earlier.

But unlike Kanye, who put on what can only be described as a huge production, Kris had opted for a more low-key proposal, writing 'Will you marry me?' in rose petals on her bed.

After Kim accepted, the couple celebrated with the Kardashian-Jenner clan during a family dinner, with cameras rolling the entire time for an episode of *Keeping Up With The Kardashians*. The ring later went under the hammer at an auction, finally selling for a cool $749,000. An as-yet unknown buyer at Christie's in New York City purchased the enormous jewel. Bidding for the diamond had begun at $200,000 at the auction, entitled 'Bright and Beautiful'.

But Kim was determined things would be different this time around. The morning after the over-the-top proposal from

Kanye, she announced that she was already getting excited about her wedding: 'Last night was truly magical!' she wrote on her blog. 'I am the luckiest girl in the world! I get to marry my best friend!'

She was on the crest of a wave after announcing her engagement, and her business empire was going from strength to strength too. Just days later she and her sisters launched a new collection for fashion label Lipsy. Kim explained how she had been inspired by major designers: That idea of casual comfort that people love inspired the fabrics – there's a lot of stretch. You know an Alaïa dress will hold and suck you in? I wanted to make pieces like that, pieces to make you feel really good about yourself,' she said. 'Valentino and Isabel Marant aren't really our style, but their influence is reflected in the collection.'

Showing off her fabulous post-baby figure in the accompanying campaign, having lost 43 pounds since giving birth, Kim added: 'The collection is inspired by the stylish women from around the world that I've had the pleasure of meeting. This is for those Lipsy girls who have as much fun with fashion as I do.

'Losing this weight has not been easy, but I did it, and that's so rewarding. I was dedicated and motivated, and for me, that paid off. This makes me feel like I have the strength to take on other challenges.'

In the interview with *People Magazine*, she admitted that she had attempted to hide the weight as best she could: 'Pregnancy for me was a lot tougher than people saw on my show or from magazines,' she said, 'so to get back to feeling like myself just makes me feel good again. It's all about feeling your best.'

With Kim back on top form, Kanye could not help but share his joy, openly referring to her as his fiancée for the very first time in public. At a concert, just before he belted out his song 'Bound 2', which is about their romance, Kanye gushed to the crowd: 'You know what song this is, right? I want to sing this song to the birthday girl that's back there right now, my fiancée.'

And although known for his often hard exterior, he was clearly showing his softer side, also sharing with the audience his words of wisdom about love: 'If you came with somebody that you love tonight, hold on so tight,' he said. 'What I'm trying to say is it's hard to find you.'

Kanye also added that Kim had helped give him a second chance at life when his mother Donda died. He said that after her passing, he had begun to spiral out of control.

But the frenzy of publicity that their engagement and the arrival of their daughter had generated had also led the couple to become a widespread target for comics. The chat show host Ellen DeGeneres was among those who started to poke fun at them on a regular basis. In one opening monologue she compared the size of Kim's 15-carat Lorraine Schwartz engagement ring to her baby daughter, North West, saying: 'He did it in a very traditional way. He got down on one knee after renting out an entire baseball stadium in San Francisco. And then gave her a 15-carat diamond ring,' she joked. 'Fifteen carats, that's bigger than their baby!'

Ellen also joked that Kanye was prompted to finally ask for

Kim's hand in marriage after seeing her sexy bathing suit selfie that the reality star had tweeted the previous week.

'That is crazy,' she said. 'I wear more than that when I am naked. Obviously Kanye saw that and thought, "Well, there's my soulmate" and decided to propose.'

Ellen also offered Kanye a piece of advice: 'I want to say congratulations to both of you, but I want to warn Kanye. You start with a stadium proposal, it's going to be hard to top,' she said.

'I don't know where he is going to go from there? I mean, next year he is going to have to rent out a bigger stadium and she is going to have to take a picture with even less clothes on.'

But the couple could not hide their happiness, and Kanye took every opportunity to tell the world how happy he was with the girl of his dreams: 'I have never loved any girl, other than my mother, as much as I love my girlfriend,' he said of Kim during an interview with San Francisco radio station KMEL.

He also revealed he is in it for the long haul with Kim: 'I'm so happy to be with her, to live this life together, and – with our relationship with God – to be able to live forever in heaven together, and also to raise a strong family that communicates truth and beauty.

'This girl is one of the No. 1 designers in the world. I don't know exactly what her numbers are, but Sears does something like $300, 400 million a year.

'She's been spending her whole check on clothes since she was sixteen, just like me,' he added.

With a typical lack of modesty, Kanye also boasted that he

and Kim were the biggest power couple of them all: 'That's the reason why both of us are the most influential,' he continued. 'I think me and my girl are extremely influential. Nah, me and my girl are the most influential.'

He went so far as to liken Kim to music mogul Jay-Z: 'One of the reasons I did *Watch the Throne* with Jay wasn't just to do a dope album, which we did. It was because Jay-Z has the best social skills of anyone that I knew at that time, and I wanted to learn from him.

'I wanted to learn how to move in a room full of vultures, just to knock the edge off and learn from Jay.

'And God has now given me another master of the social skills, my girl. She's like the No. 1 socialite in the world.'

Meanwhile Kim was being constantly quizzed about their wedding plans, but said she wanted the groom to take charge of the arrangements: 'We honestly haven't had a moment to talk about it or even breathe,' she explained, adding: 'But whatever he wants.'

And Kanye had just two words when asked for hints about the wedding: 'fighter jets', he joked, while already repeatedly referring to Kim as his 'wife'.

When asked about his over-the-top proposal in an interview with Power 106's morning radio, he admitted 'I was nervous a little bit, but more about everything being on cue.'

The infamous perfectionist also revealed it took four different jewellers and a lot of time to get Kim's 15-carat diamond engagement ring absolutely right: 'Kim knew I was eventually going to ask her to marry me,' he said. 'I just had to get that ring right. I worked with four different jewellers.

'Three rings were made and only one hit the ringer and that was Lorraine Schwartz's.

'I actually changed the ring the night before. The ring was less than four hours old when I gave it to her.'

He added that he thought 'it would be dope' to propose to Kim in the baseball stadium, explaining that the proposal went exactly to plan aside from the lights which were not 'exactly how I wanted them to be.'

And despite his famous self-confidence, Kanye was by no means certain as to Kim's response: 'I was nervous. I was talking to her cousin. I was like, "I don't know, what do you think she's going to say?" I'm not arrogant about love and feelings at all.

'I'm confident in the work I put so much work in to but this is someone else's feelings. You never know what someone else may feel at the time.

'Everybody that came in just thought it was a surprise party. As soon Kim heard the Lana Del Ray song playing, she just figured I was going to have Lana sing and we were going to have dinner. Because at a certain point she just knows I'm going to do something to turn it up. So she was expecting something awesome.'

In true confident style, Kanye also joked that his proposal put pressure on other men who are pondering the perfect way to propose 'I gotta apologise to the race of males for turning up so much,' he laughed. 'I wanted to marry that girl from the first time I saw her. Kim and I are the perfect balance.'

Kanye said he was most proud of his patience in waiting for Kim while she was with other men: 'I had to wait through a bunch of other relationships to finally get the chance,' he continued, adding he bought a mobile phone for the first time in three years just to speak and text with Kim after her split from Kris Humphries.

'I just knew I wanted her to be my girl for a long time,' he told a lengthy *On Air With Ryan Seacrest* radio interview, in which he also confirmed that Kim would take his married name, but keep Kardashian as her middle name.

'I remember I saw a picture of her and Paris Hilton, and I remember telling my boy, "Have you seen that girl Kim Kar-dijon?"'

Kanye went on to praise Kim's style credentials, adding: 'There's no way Kim Kardashian shouldn't be on the cover of *Vogue*. She's like the most intriguing woman right now. She's got Barbara Walters calling her, like, everyday,' he said. 'And collectively, we're the most influential with clothing. No one is looking at what Barack Obama is wearing. Michelle Obama cannot Instagram a bikini pic like what my girl Instagrammed the other day.'

Kanye was delighted when Kim was chosen to feature on the cover of *CR Fashion Book*, the new publication by former *French Vogue* editor Carine Roitfeld: 'Carine Roitfeld supports my girl. That's a breakthrough,' he explained. 'There's a wall of classicism that we are breaking through.'

While Kim might have been accepted by the fashion elite, Kanye's popularity had dropped by a staggering 66 per cent in the time he had been dating Kim, according to a poll by *Q Scores*, a US website which is regarded as a realistic measure of popularity and likeability. Originally Kanye had a high score of 17 among women aged between eighteen and forty-nine – before he and Kim began dating in April 2011.

And his credibility was further dented by the release of a raunchy new video for his single 'Bound 2', which featured a topless Kim straddling her fiancé on a motorbike. When it premiered on *The Ellen DeGeneres Show*, Kanye made matters worse by talking frankly about their sex life.

When Ellen asked: 'Did you want to have children? Like, did you or is this something that happened? I mean, I know how it happened, but have you been planning?' Kanye replied: 'I mean, we were just practising all the time. Practise made perfect.'

Although he discussed the physical aspects of their relationship, Kanye also opened up on what Kim means to him, adding that she had helped him through some of the most difficult moments of his life, including the death of his mother: 'She's an important person that when I was at my lowest moments I could get on the phone with her and she would make me feel like, you know, I was here for a reason and I was, you know, I had something to say and just support me through that.

'I mean, it's incredible to have a woman like that, that you know is not using you for money,' he added. 'I just have to word it like that because once you become like a multi-millionaire there's a certain type of woman out there that they go for that and they'll put on the whole act and everything.

'But to have someone that's, you know, has their own shit, and her personality is so calming. And I don't know if that's the way people would describe my personality so I don't know if I can express it enough. It's almost like people make fun of me for, like, how in love I actually am.

'I just think people are just so cool with their approach to things, you know. And also I'm trying to avoid the jump-up-on-the-couch moment, but yeah, it's just, it's good.'

And he defended the explicit tone of his music video, explaining that he would not alter anything for the sake of his young daughter: 'I'm not as concerned with the idea of profanity or nudity, it's more the messaging behind it.

'So she's going to be in the real world, so she's going to hear things and see things. I think she's got to be prepared for that.'

And although fans had been promised a 'sexy' appearance by Kim in Kanye's new music video, even those intimately acquainted with the work of the provocative rapper couldn't have been prepared for the crudely titillating four-minute film that pushed the boundaries of taste by showing the pair simulating sex against a desert background.

Fans who may have been hoping that the birth of the couple's baby daughter might have prompted the *enfant terrible* of hip-hop to draw a line in the sand when it came to gratuitous content will have been sorely disappointed by the display. As well as their explicit display of affection, the lyrics of the song hint at a lust for threesomes, casual sex and a relationship that does well to last mere months. Kanye even describes a sex act in graphic detail.

But as soon as the video was revealed, Twitter immediately blew up with a collective wail as fans rushed to brand the display 'cringe-worthy' and 'vomit inducing'. Some commentators also noted how awkward the besotted pair seem in the film, and Kim's blank face and lack of involvement in the piece other than as a wordless object of lust seemed to enrage her female fans.

She did show off the results of her weight loss since the birth of Nori, as she reclined on the bike alone at the beginning, wearing just tight trousers and a pair of high-heeled boots.

The video opens with an eagle and some galloping horses before Kanye appears alone on screen. It then cuts to him simulating riding a motorcycle in Utah's Monument Valley before viewers are treated to the first glimpse of Kim. The mountains of Yosemite also feature although those watching might be forgiven for paying more attention to Kim and Kanye's raunchy performance than the scenery.

And Kim, who dyed her hair blonde after giving birth to North, showed exactly what attracted Kanye to her as she writhed around on a motorcycle. Although bathed in shadows, it is obvious that she is naked from the waist up, as there are numerous close-ups of her breasts.

Viewers are also treated to numerous close-up shots of Kim's face as she pouts into the camera.

The video cuts between Kanye rapping, wearing black trousers and a plaid shirt, and riding the motorcycle in a tie-dyed T-shirt with Kim either behind him, her arms around his waist, straddling him or laying back on the bike with Kanye in front of her. She also showers him with kisses before the pair start making out.

But Kanye refused to be put off by friends who disapproved of his choice. In an interview with Hot 97 radio, he said: 'Ladies and gentlemen, y'all acting like this ain't the most beautiful woman of all time!' he announced. 'Arguably of human existence, the top ten of human existence.'

Kanye went on to say that dating Kim had taught him that life was about more than 'What's cool or not cool.'

'I felt like our love story is a love story for the ages,' he added. 'I felt like when we first got together it's a Romeo and Juliet kind of thing.

'Like she's a reality star and I'm a rapper and people talking about how our brands connect and it doesn't fit. And I'm just so tired of brands. It's not about branding at a certain point.'

Given he had in the past likened himself to Andy Warhol, Shakespeare, Picasso, Walt Disney, Steve Jobs and even God, it was hardly surprising.

But of course Kanye had not forgotten his daughter, North West, and went on to compare his baby girl to British royalty. Seemingly referring to Prince William, Kate Middleton, and their son, Prince George, Kanye informed New York-based radio station Power 105.1 that his 'daughter is in a position of a level of royalty like the Prince and Princess in London.'

During an interview for the station's *Breakfast Club* programme, Kanye also discussed his new controversial video for 'Bound 2', and claimed that he had wanted the film clip to look as 'trashy' and 'phoney' as possible.

When quizzed about the video, Kris Jenner added: 'I am extremely proud of my daughter Kim, and also very proud of her fiancé, Kanye West. He is extremely talented and incredibly artistic.'

The couple appeared to be having a positive effect on each

other, when Kim encouraged notoriously hot-blooded Kanye to see the funny side of spoof videos, which quickly emerged.

After actor James Franco and comedian Seth Rogen hilariously spoofed their sexually charged video, Kim took to Twitter to give it her seal of approval. She even retweeted funnyman Seth's link to the YouTube clip, titled *Bound 3*, to her over 18 million followers, and wrote: 'You nailed it!!! Sooo funny!'

The parody, which featured Seth dry-humping James as he rode a motorcycle just like Kanye, did not draw a reaction from Kanye, who is known to be somewhat sensitive when it comes to people making fun at his expense.

Not long before the parody emerged, the *Touch the Sky* star blew his top at late night talk show host Jimmy Kimmel, having taken offence at a comedy skit aimed at him.

The couple then decided to add more fuel to the fire by paying tribute to their mutual adoration with a video of their 2013 highlights set to poignant music, which Kim rather sweetly chose to post under her married-name-to-be, Kim West.

The video included Kanye's marriage proposal, along with photos and clips of the pair when they were friends and when they were more. Rihanna's hit song 'Stay' played over this first segment, as Kim wondered why the long-standing friends did not get together sooner.

In the footage she also talked of Kanye's unwavering support of her. There were clips of Kanye saying how, aside from his late mother Donda, he had never loved a woman as much as he loves Kim.

Then there was a snip of the radio interview in which he talked about Kim being one of the top ten most beautiful women of all time. Kanye and Keri Hilson's single, 'Knock You Down', kicks in for Nori's arrival and the proposal, which was fitting, given this was the song that played when Kanye proposed in San Francisco.

Despite releasing such intimate footage, it was also reported that Kim had asked her family not to share any photos of baby Nori while she was away with Kanye. She had left her daughter in the care of her mother, Kris, and sisters, Kourtney and Khloe, while she attended Paris Fashion Week with her boyfriend. And she instructed them to be extra-cautious about the pictures they shared on Twitter and Instagram while she was out of the country.

A source told gossip website *NaughtyButNiceRob.com*: 'Kim does not think for one minute that her mom or sisters would try to sell pictures of North. Her concern was that everyone in the family loves to post pictures of what they are doing all the time on Twitter, and that this is something that she does not want to happen while she is away.

'She knows her daughter is in safe hands, not very discreet hands, but safe!'

Kim admitted that Kanye had encouraged her to be more low-key. She said during an interview on *The Today Show*: 'When you spend time with someone, you learn things from them, so I see what [his] views are in wanting to be private, so that's a choice we make together as a family just in how we're gonna raise our kid.'

Instead, Kim was focusing on regaining her pre-baby

curves. As well as enduring more than 100 squats every single morning, she had hired a personal chef and trainer to keep her in perfect shape as she accompanied Kanye on his 'Yeezus' Tour.

'She's got a trainer on tour with her and Kanye, and a chef to keep her meals carb-free,' a source told *People.com*. 'With the exception of some cheat days, because she is realistic now, she sticks with it!'

It emerged that Kanye was paying $250,000 for Kim's 'glam squad', having also arranged to have her hairdresser, make-up artist and stylist on call to join them whenever they were needed, since Kim refused to use anyone else's services.

A source told *RadarOnline.com*: 'Kanye has told Kim he will spare no expense to make her look ready to go to a major photo shoot whenever she desires. So, Kim's hair stylist, make-up artist, and stylist, all based in Los Angeles, are on call 24/7, ready to get on a private jet to be whisked to her location.

'Kim only trusts her team to make her look gorgeous and doesn't want to work with outsiders. This doesn't come cheap, and Kanye will shell out $250,000 just while he is on tour for Kim's glam squad. The money doesn't mean anything to him because Kanye wants his lady to look perfect.'

Kanye reportedly did not get upset about Kim's image bills – because he was spending even more money on himself. The source added: 'Kim loves that money is no issue ever with Kanye. He never balks at how much money Kim spends.

'The truth is that Kanye spends a lot more than Kim does on clothes, accessories and cars. They are a perfect match for each other.'

Kim has always prioritised her carefully maintained looks. In *Kardashian Konfidential* she told that she was all about clean living, which she believes is the source of all beauty.

She talked further about the magic of professional stylists, saying not only do they overhaul your physical figure, they totally change the way you feel about yourself. When Kim knows the difference between looking good in the mirror and looking good on a camera lens which can catch unflattering angles and blow up parts of the body one might not necessarily want enlarged.

Kim's 'glam squad' even become close friends in her personal life – when you spend hours every week in the hair salon, or getting your make-up done you come to confide in them and gossip with them – plus, they're the only people that see her first thing in the morning without any cosmetic attention!

Kim started to take another leaf out of Kanye's book, by regularly rewarding her expanding team of staff, and made a point of tipping a restaurant valet $100 for parking her car.

'She is sending super-expensive floral arrangements to everyone who helps her,' a source revealed. 'It's Kim's bizarre new way of expressing gratitude. She picked it up from Kanye. Kim's new thing is to send everybody who works with her, even her manicurist, these ridiculously expensive flower arrangements the day after she sees them,' the source added.

Kim had been using 'florist to the stars' Eric Buterbaugh, who is a favourite with actress Demi Moore: 'Kim has been testing out a number of LA-based florists,' the source went on.

It was suggested that Kim was trying various florists in anticipation of her wedding, which she had started planning soon after Kanye popped the question. Kim has long been a lover of over-the-top floral arrangements. She shared a photo of an elaborate bouquet of rare flowers from brother Robon her birthday. Weeks later she showed off a lavish bouquet of roses from her fiancé with the caption, 'I love you'.

Despite the couple's happiness, Kanye became a suspect in a battery investigation after an alleged altercation with a man in a chiropractor's office.

The unidentified eighteen-year-old man told Beverly Hills police that he wanted to press charges against the star, and law enforcement sources in LA confirmed that Kanye was officially a suspect and that the matter had been referred to the LA County DA for possible prosecution.

The dramatic altercation supposedly unfolded as Kim entered a furniture store and the man began shouting shocking racist abuse at her.

Deeply perturbed, Kim then is said to have phoned Kanye to tell him what was happening. Within minutes, Kanye arrived to meet up with Kim and learn face-to-face what had happened. After the incident, the boy claimed to have been assaulted. Beverly Hills police officers arrived on the scene but Kim and Kanye had already left.

'Kanye was named as a suspect by the victim as well as several witnesses. He had left prior to our arrival, and detectives are currently investigating,' Beverly Hills Police Sgt. George DeMarois told the *New York Daily News*.

Already Kanye was facing charges of battery and attempted grand theft after an earlier altercation with a photographer at Los Angeles Airport. Photographer Daniel Ramos had told police that he was taking pictures of Kanye when the suspect attacked him. Rob Wilcox, spokesman for the Los Angeles city attorney's office, said each of the two charges carried a maximum sentence of six months in jail.

But eventually Kanye was sentenced to attend 24 private anger management sessions. Although Ramos had been taken to hospital for his injuries, Kanye's lawyer entered a no contest pleas on his behalf, to a count of battery. The judge ruled that the rapper be sentenced to two years' probation, and must attend an anger management course.

Although Kanye is known for scowling at photographers, Kim has always taken the attention coolly in her stride, and appears to embrace the downsides of her fame.

She has always maintained that she is lucky to be able to travel, meet new people, dress to the nines and live a full-tilt luxury lifestyle. But like any job, celebrity comes at a price, and as well as suffering from burnout you run the risk of developing a critically swollen ego.

But Kim was not prepared to let anything or anyone ruin her happiness when she appeared on *The Ellen DeGeneres Show*, proudly sharing several previously unseen photos of North during an interview. And she gushed about parenthood, revealing that the seven-month-old is the perfect baby: 'She changes all the time,' said Kim. 'One day she'll look like Kanye, one day she'll look like me. It's so crazy.

'And her personality is so cute. She is really calm and really quiet.'

When asked whether she had always wanted to have children, Kim admitted she: 'Always wanted about six!'

'After having her I would have a million,' she continued, though she revealed the pregnancy was far from smooth-sailing and not something she wanted to repeat anytime soon.

'The pregnancy, I wouldn't really wish that upon anyone. Anyone,' she insisted.

'Then you can adopt,' Ellen suggested.

Kim was quick to amend her statement, saying: 'It's all worth it in the end, so I would definitely suffer through that, but pregnancy was not a good experience for me. At all.

'Women who say that it's a beautiful thing, they are lying. They are lying to you. I'm telling you. Kourtney said that, my mum said that. I was literally giving birth and I looked at my mum and I said, "I'm going to get you a medal. You deserve everything."

'My labour was easy, but just the whole pregnancy was so... I had a few medical issues, so it was really tough, and I gained a lot of weight.'

Kim has struggled with her weight in the past, but told how she learnt to accept her body shape: 'We can tone our bodies, shrink them, stretch them, whatever,' she said. 'But in the end, we'll still have the same basic bodies we were born with, even if they're firmer, slimmer, and more flexible bodies.'

Kim went on to admit that she started 'hysterically crying' after she began reading the classic pregnancy advice book *What To Expect When You're Expecting*, which sister Kourtney gave her, saying it 'made it so much worse'.

'It was really hard mentally on me,' she admitted. But the reality TV star had the audience in fits of laughter as she insisted her hormones did not get the better of her during the challenging pregnancy: 'I was actually really calm, my hormones weren't really going crazy. Well, I don't think – you might want to ask Kanye or someone!' she chuckled. 'I think with all of the medical issues – I had pre-eclampsia, which was really tough, I had to deliver early... But I wouldn't take any of it back because I have the most adorable, sweetest baby in the world,' she smiled.

Kim shared a cute photo of the infant riding on her dad's shoulders during what she described as an 'intense Monopoly game' while vacationing in Utah, as she revealed just how hands-on a parent Kanye is with his daughter.

'He is honestly the most amazing dad,' Kim said of her fiancé. 'He loves her so much. He just left to go out of town, so I send him a picture and video every day. He's like, "She grew up so much!" and I'm like, "Babe, it's been one day. You haven't seen her in a day. Not a lot has changed." But he really is a hands-on dad.

'He's not a diaper-changing kind of guy, and that's okay,' she added. 'He would if it's an emergency. But I love that time. I know it sounds crazy, but I love my time with her when she's on the changing table. She tries to talk so much and I really enjoy that bonding time when I'm with her.'

Kim then shared two more photos from the day before, when she was trying bow headbands on the photogenic youngster: 'She doesn't wear a lot of bows and my niece Penelope [Disick] wears so many headbands, so I was trying all these bows on her and she really liked them, so I think she's going to start wearing some bows,' said Kim.

Ellen reminded the star, rather awkwardly, that the last time she was on the show – two years earlier – she was performing a wedding vow renewal for Kim and her then-husband Kris Humphries. 'A lot has changed since then,' Kim stated.

Swiftly changing the subject, she shared her joy about Kanye's over-the-top marriage proposal: 'That was probably one of the only times I've been surprised,' she admitted. 'I usually know everything and I was actually so shocked that he kept that a secret from me. And it was such a good secret.

'But he's also so passionate about birthdays. That's his thing.'

Kim insisted that up until the last minute, she had no idea Kanye was proposing, thinking it was simply an elaborate birthday bash: 'I truly didn't know it was happening until he got down on one knee,' she said.

But while Ellen gave Kim superstar treatment, she was on the receiving end of a savage attack from another TV personality just days later. Comedienne Joan Rivers sparked controversy when she criticised Kim's baby, branding North 'ugly' and 'desperately in need of a waxing'.

As part of a stand-up comedy routine Joan explained how she had met the tot when Kim brought her into the offices of the *E!* television network, where Joan hosts *Fashion Police*.

Joan told her audience: 'That baby is ugly. I've never seen a six-month-old so desperately in need of a waxing.'

When Kim first revealed a full-face photo of her child on social media, she had been inundated by harsh comments suggesting that she had waxed the baby's perfectly groomed brows. Taking to Twitter to defend her child's appearance, Kim wrote: 'Do people really think I would wax my daughter's eyebrows so young? Come on, I'd wait until she's at least 2½!

'I'm kidding!!! It's pretty sick for people to insinuate that I would wax my daughter's eyebrows. They are thick, natural and amazing!'

Joan's joke did not go down well with Kanye, who is fiercely protective of his daughter and vowed shortly before her birth last June that he was determined she would enjoy a normal childhood and not let people take advantage of her. He said: 'This is my baby, this isn't America's baby.'

Explaining his fatherly duties further, he added: 'One of the things was to be protective, that I would do anything to protect my child or my child's mother. As simple as that.'

Kanye was also upset when Kim dressed North in a two-piece swimsuit to take her for her first dip in a pool. Kim told Ellen: 'Kanye is a little uncomfortable with North wearing a bikini. I tried it once and it did not go over well. It has to be a one-piece.'

CHAPTER 9

ENJOYING THEIR ENGAGEMENT

Although engaged and happily planning their wedding, Kim and Kanye were still living with with Kim's mother Kris Jenner in Hidden Hills while they waited for work on their palatial Bel Air mansion to be completed.

And Kanye begged his fiancée for some alone time at the start of 2014 after enduring a New Year's holiday with the entire Kardashian clan. During an appearance on *Jimmy Kimmel Live*, where she showed off her incredible post-baby figure in a cropped top and clinging skirt, Kim explained: 'We spent New Year's in a condo with my mother and Kanye said, "Can we just have three days to ourselves without your family?" so we went to Paris.

'We will be getting married, this summer hopefully, in Paris. It's our second home. We spend so much time there, we have an apartment there. I'm not telling where or the date but it's definitely Paris.

'It was too far for North to come so my mom and my sisters all looked after her. He's moved in with me, my mom, two little sisters so that's why we needed to get away.

'We live with my mom because our house is being worked on right now.'

It also emerged that the pair were apparently having problems with the massive home renovation project: 'He's impossible to please,' revealed a friend of the couple.

'She just wants to be settled,' the source told *Life & Style*. 'Not squatting in someone else's house. The house has a long way to go before they can move in. It's frustrating for Kim.

'He's a total snob when it comes to style, design and architecture – he thinks nothing of changing direction midway and starting over.'

The $11million mansion had been gutted to make room for a man cave for the rapper, as well as a new gym, a movie theatre, bowling alley and basketball court.

Another source of nervous energy at the same time was the wedding, which was expected to be a lavish affair.

'Everything will be very ornate, from the invitations to the cake,' a source told *inTouch* magazine. 'They want something very grand. It's already become a circus.

'And they want an A-list guest list – think Jay-Z and Beyoncé – that will have to be flown in by private jet. They want the craziest, most elaborate wedding experience anybody has ever had,' added a friend.

Although they were prevented from throwing the bash

at their dream location, the Palace of Versailles, apparently because Palace officials thought the couple were not an appropriate fit for the venue, Kim and Kanye started to consider a number of other, equally grand castles close to the French capital, including Château d'Ussé.

The insider went on to suggest that Kim wanted to wear a tiara like Kate Middleton's Cartier choice for her big day: Kanye wants them to wear matching couture.

'They want it to be as opulent and extravagant as possible and have zero consideration about cost,' added the source.

The price tag for the day was already estimated to be around $30m, but the stars would not have to pay all of that. If the event were to be televised, the TV network would undoubtedly foot most of that bill. With the ratings for *Keeping Up With The Kardashians* continuing to slide, producer Ryan Seacrest was said to be looking for something to kick up the numbers. But Kanye did not want to broadcast their nuptials.

And he was still against the idea of putting his daughter on TV. 'Kim really wants to put North on the show. Viewers and fans of the show want to see Kim interact with her daughter, and how she is as a mother,' revealed a source. 'Kim has always been an open book with her fans, but once Kanye came on the scene, that all changed. Kanye shuts Kim down whenever she brings it up.'

The rapper doesn't want his only child to ever pop up on the *E!* show, the source added, because he believes reality TV is 'tacky'.

'He doesn't want North on display. He will be very happy when Kim is done with the show,' explained the insider. But he was weighing up the possibility of allowing his over-the-top wedding to Kim to be filmed, according to *Radar*.

Viewers had not been tuning into the reality show as much as they used to. The season nine premiere in January 2014 drew only 2.56 million viewers, almost 500,000 less than the premiere of season eight in June 2013.

Seacrest, who is also the host of *American Idol*, had personally asked Kim to bring her first child onto the show, showing just how anxious he was to help win new fans. He is very close to the entire family, even being a part of Khloe's 2009 wedding to Lamar Odom.

Kim's sister Kourtney had allowed her son Mason – who gets his own pay check for his services – to appear not just on *Keeping Up With The Kardashians* but also *Kourtney & Khloe Take Miami* as well as other spinoffs.

And while the newly engaged couple debated over whether North should appear on air, they were having to deal with yet more dubious allegations that Kanye was seen getting into an elevator at The Dream Hotel in Miami, Florida 'on January 5th or 4th' with Gabriella Amore, a pretty brunette who is a dead ringer for Kim, according to an unidentified woman who talked to websites *The Dirty* and *TabRag* in late January 2014.

Kanye immediately fired off a response, calling the story 'ridiculous', adding that he was not even in that city at the time of the alleged sighting. The *Yeezus* singer did have a tour stop in Miami in early December, but on 4 January he was spotted running errands with Kim in Beverly Hills.

'Kanye was never even in Miami during this period. He

was on vacation with his family,' the singer's representative said. On New Year's Eve the performer was in Utah with his fiancée.

But Kim knew that Kanye had not strayed, and the couple returned to the business of planning their big day. Unlike most grooms, Kanye was determined to put his stamp of approval on every detail – right down to the two couture gowns he wanted his fiancée to wear. The date was also brought forward because Kim wished to plan her second pregnancy and did not want to be expecting when she walked down the aisle.

'The goal now is to start trying after they get married,' explained a source, who added that Kim did not want the wedding to be as big as her first, which was attended by more than 500 guests. But Kanye appeared to have other ideas: 'Kim isn't totally pumped about a huge wedding,' the insider told *Life & Style Weekly*. 'But she's going along with it.

'Kim and Kanye will be in handcrafted headpieces he commissioned for them. He thinks he and Kim are royalty.'

As well as planning to use a castle as their venue, the couple were also thought to be keen to have big name stars like Stevie Wonder and John Legend to perform.

And while the plans continued to gather pace, Kanye continued to lavish his fiancée with expensive gifts, with grand displays of affection – such as filling an entire room with long-stem red rose bouquets for Valentine's Day.

'A thousand roses!' the thirty-three-year-old reality star tweeted with delight. 'Nothing better than being with my love on Valentine's Day! Happy Vday dolls!'

Kim shared three Instagram snaps of her romantic day with

the rapper, but then in a new X-rated new rap on a remix of Beyoncé and Jay-Z's hit 'Drunk In Love', Kanye charmingly revealed how he knew Kim would be his wife after she performed a certain act in the bedroom.

In the explicit rap, Kanye revealed: 'I impregnated your mouth, girl, that's when I knew you could be my spouse, girl.'

And Kanye continued to display the strength of their relationship with his extreme interest in Kim's career, which, according to a source close to the family, actually led to butting heads with Kim's momager Kris over the direction of his fiancée's business interests.

A source told *Radar Online*: 'His goal is to get people to respect Kim and take her seriously – it's basically the same kind of thing he did when he was launching his rap career after being known primarily as a producer.'

The insider went on to claim that Kanye was instrumental in helping Kim announce her latest project – a range of 'super affordable' baby clothes, named 'Kardashian Kids', to be launched in March 2014.

That announcement followed a string of commercially viable endorsements and business ventures, among them a cosmetics line, clothing collections for Sears and Lipsy, sunglasses and several fragrances, not to mention the family's chain of Dash boutiques.

But despite Kanye's involvement in the business side of Kim's career apparently didn't extend to speaking out during the fall-out when it was claimed that he and Kim might have dressed up their extravagant engagement for an episode of *Keeping Up With The Kardashians*.

When the long-awaited proposal scene hit screens in the US, eagle-eyed viewers spotted that Kim had been wearing her glittering Lorraine Schwartz 15-carat diamond ring in the previous week's episode – 'A Surprise Engagement Pt. 1'. Kim was seen wearing the dazzling band in a scene that showed her putting away clothes for the couple's baby daughter, while her sisters, Kourtney and Khloe, talked about her behind her back. This is despite the engagement allegedly happening a whole week later.

This could simply have been a case of an unfortunate mishap in the editing suite, but it wouldn't be the first time *Keeping Up With The Kardashians* bosses had been clever with footage for the *E!* fly-on-the-wall show.

A spokesperson for Bunim/Murray Productions told the *MailOnline*: 'The footage of Kim folding baby clothes, while wearing her engagement ring, although filmed after the proposal, was a better fit for the first episode of the two-part engagement special because we wanted part two to focus on the surprise that was to come.'

The latest controversy came amid falling viewing figures, with some shows averaging around 2.4million – half a million fewer viewers than weekly episodes during peak seasons. But in spite of the somewhat lacklustre ratings, the *E!* series was renewed for a further three seasons in a deal worth an alleged $40million.

The fans that did tune in were finally able to see the moment the rapper asked Kim to be his wife, in all of its extravagant glory. With roman candles burning, the rapper told Kim: 'I just want to know.'

But the happy couple would not let anything ruin their plans to marry in May 2014, and in an emotionally charged interview on *Late Night With Seth Meyers*, Kanye said: 'My approach to life has changed.'

He added: 'There were times [after my mum's death], I would put my life at risk. I didn't have something to live for. Now I have two very special people to live for, a whole family to live for, a whole world to live for.'

Kim was happier than ever too, despite an onslaught of abuse, which she seemed to face every time she went out. When she attended a glitzy ball in Austria, she came in for a barrage of criticism after she left early, having been involved in an alleged race row.

TMZ revealed that Kim stormed out of the Vienna Ball after she was approached by a white male working at the event with a 'black face' began to mimic her fiancé. The site also claimed that Kim – who stayed for around an hour and a half after the incident before leaving – finally made her exit when another man made a racial remark.

TMZ reported that a man offered to dance with her 'if the orchestra played N****rs in Vienna', referencing Kanye's song, 'N****rs In Paris'.

But there was some good news for the couple, when they fulfilled their dream of appearing on the cover of *Vogue* magazine in the spring of 2014. For years Kim had longed to be featured in the iconic fashion bible, but her rumoured strained relationship with editor Anna Wintour had always been seen as the reason she was not chosen as a cover star.

'Kim has wanted this for so long, she is beyond happy,' a

source told *Us Weekly* magazine. 'She doesn't listen to what other people think.'

In the shoot, which took place over two days in LA in late January, Kim wore a selection of different white wedding-inspired gowns. North was also involved in the shoot and posed with her parents for a selection of images by famous celebrity photographer Annie Leibovitz.

Although there was a furious backlash from *Vogue* fans, who felt putting Kim and Kanye on the cover was a huge mistake, Anna Wintour spoke out publicly to defend her controversial decision. She insisted that Kanye had not begged her, as some critics had suggested, and maintained it had been entirely her own idea.

'Part of the pleasure of editing *Vogue*, one that lies in a long tradition of this magazine, is being able to feature those who define the culture at any given moment, who stir things up, whose presence in the world shapes the way it looks and influences the way we see it,' she wrote in her editorial. 'I think we can all agree on the fact that that role is currently being played by Kim and Kanye to a T. Or perhaps that should be to a K?

'As for the cover, my opinion is that it is both charming and touching, and it was, I should add, entirely our idea to do it; you may have read that Kanye begged me to put his fiancée on *Vogue*'s cover. He did nothing of the sort. The gossip might make better reading, but the simple fact of the matter is that it isn't true.'

Whilst an insider apparently told *Star* magazine that while Ms Wintour thought Kanye was 'terrific', it was suggested by a source that Kim was shunned from the Met Gala in 2012. While Kanye attended the New York party in a bow tie and suit, his girlfriend stayed at home in LA and tweeted about the star-studded event instead.

However, Kim was among the guests the following year.

But despite the alleged clash of personalities, Kanye was undoubtedly a friend of Anna Wintour's, especially given that he runs a high-end fashion label of his own. He even gave the *Vogue* editor-in-chief a shout-out in the lyrics of his song 'Cold'.

Kim had graced the July/August issue of *Vogue Italia* the previous year, however, sporting a sexy pixie haircut.

Many fans of the fashion bible were appalled by the April cover of *US Vogue*, with some even cancelling their subscriptions, including actress Sarah Michelle Gellar, who tweeted: 'Well… I guess I'm cancelling my Vogue subscription. Who is with me???'

Her boycott was retweeted more than 8,000 times and favourited by more than 11,000 people.

Vogue's Facebook page was also inundated with hundreds of disapproving messages.

'I'm done with Vogue. Subscription cancelled sick to death of Kanye and Kim used to be high fashion, your standards have been highly compromised!!!!!!' wrote one commentator.

And the *New York Post* claimed that sales had been poor, and the issue had sold less than the previous year's Michelle Obama cover. Josh Gary, vice president at Mag Net Data, told the *Post*: 'The trends for Kim K. are definitely better than the prior month with Rihanna, to the tune of 20 per cent better.'

But he added: 'I'd argue that if you peg last year's Michelle Obama at 269,000, this issue will net out around 250,000.'

That figure is considerably lower than the initial 400,000–500,000 estimate that emerged when the magazine went on sale.

Kim described her first *Vogue* cover as 'a dream come true', and could not hide her joy at her major fashion coup, tweeting: 'This is such a dream come true!!! Thank you @VogueMagazine for this cover! O M GGGGGG!!! I can't even breathe!'

The cover line introduced the piece as: 'Kim & Kanye: Their fashionable life and surreal times. #worldsmosttalked aboutcouple'.

It was the first time a hash tag was used on the *Vogue* cover and referred to Kim's huge social media presence – at the time she had around 20 million Twitter followers.

CHAPTER 10

WEDDING PLANS

'We're having a super, super-small, intimate wedding,' Kim insisted in an interview with Ryan Seacrest. 'As we go along, we're realizing we want it to be smaller and more intimate than people are imagining and thinking.'

And in her *Vogue* interview Kim reiterated that she wanted it to be nothing like her previous wedding to Kris Humphries: 'People are probably assuming we're going to have this massive wedding. And I think that it will be – but intimate. Two hundred people – just all of our closest friends – a special night for us and all the people who really love us and have supported us.'

However, the hype surrounding the eagerly anticipated nuptials seemed to suggest the wedding was going to be among the most extravagant parties of all time.

At the end of April 2014 the couple were in Paris sorting

out last-minute preparations, including booking a mock seventeenth-century French château for their big day. Kim was pictured visiting Château Louis XIV, built just six years earlier in Louveciennes, 14 miles outside of Paris.

According to sources, Kim and Kanye planned to imitate Kate Middleton and Prince William's famous kiss on the balcony of Buckingham Palace, in front of their 200 guests.

'Architects have quoted £200,000 to build a temporary balcony,' a source told *Grazia* magazine, adding that the château even has an underwater room beneath the moat: 'Kim has fallen in love with the place.'

Meanwhile Kanye spent the last few days before the wedding finalising hire of the Eiffel Tower for a private dinner. The couple had spoken to officials about exclusively hiring both of the landmark's restaurants, 58 Tour Eiffel and Le Jules Verne, as well as the beautiful conference room at the top of the famous tower, for a rehearsal dinner and cocktails the night before the wedding.

'They want to give their guests a real taste of Paris,' explained the source. 'Kanye is also in talks to hold a spectacular fireworks display to rival the lightshow at the London Olympics.'

The groom also took on the job of ordering the drinks for the reception, including £18,000 bottles of bespoke vintage champagne, £15,000 bottles of Pinot Noir wine and a £120,000 Hennessy Beauté du Siècle cognac – the most expensive in the world.

It was also being reported that Kim planned to wear three different gowns over the course of the day. During the trip to Paris she was seen visiting top designers Balmain, Lanvin and Riccardo Tisci at Givenchy, sparking a frenzy of fevered speculation that they might be her chosen couturiers. 'Kim had final fittings including a dress Kanye had been overseeing the design of at Givenchy,' added the source.

Kanye also reportedly had his final suit fitting at tailors Cifonelli, and as Kim left Paris she added to the pre-wedding excitement by tweeting the cover of a children's storybook called *Fancy Nancy and the Wedding of the Century*.

Kanye had previously suggested that they wanted to get married at the Palace of Versailles, saying in an interview: 'We could get the Hall of Mirrors or something,' referring to Versailles' central passageway, but in the end permission was not granted for them to hire the world's most famous château.

As well as putting the finishing touches to her outfits for the wedding, Kim was also spending every spare moment getting herself in peak physical condition. She even jetted out to Phuket in Thailand with her sister Khloe for a bizarre procedure called 'butt, face and breast slapping'. Costing £200 for each 15-minute session, the treatment is said to erase wrinkles, shrink pores and tighten the skin, using slapping, kneading and massaging techniques. Meanwhile 'butt slapping' is said to firm the bottom. A recent study by the Thai Health Ministry into 'breast slapping' found that vigorous massage shifts fat from one area to another and left the volunteers' breasts measurably bigger!

'Kim did quite a lot of reading into these natural techniques online before her trip, and she had three 15-minute treatments of each while she was there,' said a source.

Other sources said that Kanye had banned Kim from having any invasive surgery, after his mother had died following cosmetic surgery.

'She wants her skin to glow on her wedding day, and her body has to be as pert as possible. Kim has also indulged in placenta hair, face and body masks which boost collagen – and she feels better than ever,' reported *Grazia*.

During the Kardashians' stay in Thailand, Kim was also said to have slept in a corset every night to ensure her waist would be as small as possible when she slipped into her three gowns. This dangerous technique has been proven to shrink the waist and ensure a more defined shape, although long term it can cause digestive and lung problems. The source in *Grazia* also reported 'Kim wants her figure to look absolutely perfect on her wedding day. Wearing a corset at night is extremely uncomfortable but has a proven record of results, and with six weeks to go, Kim is up for trying anything.'

But it was not just her waist that Kim was concerned about. The star, who was spending at least £75,000 a head to ensure each of her 200 guests had a party to remember, was said to be desperate to shed as much weight as possible in time for the big day itself. Already she had lost more than three stone following the Atkins Diet since the birth of her daughter North, but in April Kim admitted on website *MobioInsider* 'I actually saw I gained some weight back when I saw pictures of myself recently and started it again. I had to check myself. I now work out five times a week and try to eat as healthily as possible.'

Kim told friends she was intent on losing a further 10

pounds and reaching a US size zero by the time she walked down the aisle – at the time she was a US size 2, a 6 in the UK.

'The Atkins Diet has been a triumph for Kim, but she has stopped following it in the last few weeks in order to shock her body into more weight loss,' the source told *Grazia*. 'She had started to plateau and Kim says she won't walk down the aisle until she's a size zero.'

In Phuket Kim carefully limited her calorie intake to just 1,200 a day, with Thai herbal teas for breakfast, papaya juice with turmeric for lunch and then a small, healthy dinner. She was also working out for two hours a day and had lymphatic massages, intensive sweats and slimming body wraps, which she continued after returning home to LA.

Kim lost 56 pounds in the six months following the birth of baby North, with a low-carb, high-fat ketogenic-style Atkins diet. Her daily menu consisted of between 1,800 and 2,200 calories and a carb intake limited to less than 60 grams. She combined proteins such as fish, chicken and meat with healthy fats like olive oil, avocados and nuts, low-starch vegetables and low-glycaemic fruits. She had also been exercising rigorously, combining cardio exercise with body-sculpting calisthenics.

And according to a source talking to *People Magazine*, Kim was also making last-minute visits to Epione of Beverly Hills, a cosmetic laser centre featured on *Keeping Up With The Kardashians*. Kim televised a trip to have laser treatment on her breasts but the centre also carry out laser hair removal treatment (something she uses) and Botox, which she's admitted to trying in the past.

The couple, who are among the wealthiest A-listers on the

planet, had been putting together a multi-million pound pre-nuptial agreement in advance of their wedding, which was said to include a 'fat clause' and an 'infidelity clause'. 'Kim and Kanye have a lot to lose, should they split up,' said the source. 'Their lawyers have drawn up an extensive list, which includes a clause stating a weight limit for both of them to stick within, and Kim isn't allowed to go under a certain weight and lose her curves.

'They have thought of everything when it comes to this wedding, and with not long to go, plans are full steam ahead.'

According to reports, the couple were struggling to keep the guest list down to around 200 close friends and family, in a determined bid to make it completely different from Kim's last wedding, which had featured in a four-hour, two-part special of *Keeping Up With The Kardashians*. There were also reports swirling around the same time that the nuptials would have to be postponed because lawyers were still hashing out their pre-nup.

With a combined wealth of $160m, and a huge amount of assets to be divided should the couple ever split up, a source told *TMZ* that they were both insisting everything was done properly: 'The current negotiations are friendly. There's no fighting. There's just a lot to work out, and it got complicated by the fact that Kanye recently changed management.'

Kanye dumping his old management company and signing with Jay-Z's Roc Nation instead had caused the delays to the pre-nup.

It was also revealed that the couple had chosen a stellar night for their wedding – an actual meteor shower was due the same evening! According to Russian astronomer Mikhail Maslov, the earth was set to pass through the tail of Comet 209P/LINEAR between 7:00 and 8:00 UT on 24 May 2014. He predicted that this would result in a meteor storm producing between 100 and 400 meteors an hour.

At the time it was being suggested that the couple would marry in a private civil service near their Los Angeles home, followed by a gala wedding celebration in France – they could not legally marry there since they had not been French residents.

But Kim was growing tired of all the false wedding rumours, and took to Twitter to answer a few of the allegations, saying: 'Seeing so many different reports, not gonna start disputing them all but a few I want to straighten out.'

She then tweeted:

1. We are not married yet!
2. We are not filming our wedding for *Keeping Up With The Kardashians*. You will see everything leading up til and after! As much as we would love to share these memories on camera, we've decided to keep this close to our heart & share thru photos. Privacy is our main priority.
3. No guest list has been released. Seeing fake ones. Especially not 1600 people invited like I just read. It's VERY small & intimate.
4. Seeing fake wedding dress pics of me. No one has seen my dress! Those photos are old or photo shopped.

And finally – 'That's it! Unless you hear it from us please don't believe nonsense!'

In the final few days before the wedding Kim was seen with her friend, tennis player Serena Williams, visiting Lanvin and Givenchy for final dress fittings. She had made sure she was in the best shape of her life, and showed off her chiselled abs in a revealing Instagram photo, with the caption: 'Just finished my morning workout'.

According to *Life & Style* magazine, Kanye had wanted Jay-Z to be his best man. An insider said, 'Jay is Kanye's closest friend so he wants him to be best man. Jay agreed initially but had one condition – under no circumstances can there be any reality TV shows filming him, his wife Beyoncé or daughter Blue Ivy during the ceremony.'

Other friends were also sworn to secrecy about details of the celebration, including Kim's best pal, Jonathan Cheban, who admitted he was struggling to come up with the perfect gift for the couple who have everything. He said in an interview on *E! News*: 'It's very hard,' he said. 'It's going to take me the next two weeks to find them a gift and hopefully I'll get it in time. But I think with a couple like that it's got to be something monogrammable, something very special because they have everything.'

Even Kris Jenner claimed she knew nothing about the couple's wedding plans: 'Kim and Kanye have done this all on their own and they've had the best time planning it and I know nothing,' she told *E!*

Two weeks before the wedding, Kim held her Parisian themed bridal shower at The Peninsula hotel in Beverly Hills. Wearing a strapless white dress, the shower was filmed for *Keeping Up With The Kardashians*. Kim's best friend, the singer Ciara, and other guests, including twin actresses Malika and Khadijah Haqq, model Brittny Gastineau, fashion designer Rachel Roy and *Real Housewives* reality TV star Larsa Pippen, were treated to white rose centrepieces on every table, a small white chocolate Eiffel Tower statue was placed on each guest's plate, and they were served brioche French toast. Fashion designer Rachel Roy uploaded a photo of her table setting, which featured a white, ceramic Eiffel Tower and a box of Ladurée macaroons. She captioned the elegant pic: 'Oui! Saturday wedding shower'.

Kim also released photos taken in a personalised photo booth of herself and her friends, with each picture captioned 'Kanye hearts Kim'.

Hosts of the shower, Kim's mother Kris and sisters Khloe and Kourtney, decided to change venues because the owner of The Beverly Hills Hotel, the Sultan of Brunei, Hassanal Bolkiah, has implemented a law in his country that includes death by stoning of gay people. It was the latest in a string of celebrity protests against properties owned by the Sultan's Dorchester Collection. The following day Kim celebrated her first Mother's Day in style – waking up to an extravagant wall of roses, hydrangeas and peonies from her fiancé in the back garden of the Jenner mansion in Hidden Hills. She even took a video of the lavish floral arrangement to show the world just how fabulous it was. During the clip her daughter North, aged 11 months, could be heard saying 'Dada', to which she answered back, 'Yeah, Daddy.' But according to a report from *Us Weekly*, she had yet to say 'Mama'.

Kim also posted a photo of herself as a baby, as well as a black-and-white photo of herself holding North as she lay on her back in a white dress. The shot had been taken in the child's bedroom as a Lucite crib could be seen in the background, as well as North's toys, including a stuffed giraffe.

'This little girl has changed my world in more ways than I ever could have imagined!' she captioned the picture. 'Being a mom is the most rewarding feeling in the world! Happy Mother's Day to all of the moms out there!'

Meanwhile, Kanye posted a moving tribute to his late mother – a photo of sunrays coming through clouds with the caption, 'Hi Mom'.

Kim's mother Kris posted a photo of herself smiling in a photo booth, alongside her own mother, Mary Jo Campbell.

But even though she was busy with last-minute wedding preparations, Kim still found time to blog about a serious subject close to her heart – racism and discrimination in America.

She wrote: 'I never knew how much being a mom would change me. It's amazing how one little person and the love I have for her has brought new meaning to every moment. What once seemed so important, now feels insignificant.'

Surprising readers with her passion and eloquence on the subject, she continued: 'It's a beautiful thing to feel and experience so much more, but with that beauty comes a flip side – seeing through my daughter's eyes the side of life that isn't always so pretty.

'To be honest, before I had North, I never really gave racism or discrimination a lot of thought. It is obviously a topic that Kanye is passionate about, but I guess it was easier for me to believe that it was someone else's battle. But recently, I've read and personally experienced some incidents that have sickened me and made me take notice. I realize that racism and discrimination are still alive, and just as hateful and deadly as they ever have been.'

She added that she felt a responsibility as a public figure and mother to help all children not 'grow up in a world where they are judged by the colour of their skin, or their gender, or their sexual orientation.'

'I want my daughter growing up in a world where love for one another is the most important thing. So the first step I'm taking is to stop pretending like this isn't my issue or my problem, because it is, it's everyone's,' she added.

'Because the California teenager who was harassed and killed by his classmates for being gay, the teenage blogger in Pakistan who was shot on her school bus for speaking out in favour of women's rights, the boy in Florida who was wrongly accused of committing a crime and ultimately killed because of the colour of his skin, they are all someone's son and someone's daughter and it is our responsibility to give them a voice.'

Perhaps predictably, she faced a storm of criticism following her blog post as she was mocked for not appearing to have taken racism seriously before.

As well as the fallout from that, she also had to deal with spurious rumours concerning her fiancé's relationship with seventeen-year-old singer Pia Mia Perez, although the teenage songbird finally decided to set the record straight, weeks after the allegations first emerged.

In May 2014, a source claimed that Pia and Kanye had been flirting with one another after he had taken her under his wing, mentoring her about both music and fashion.

'Kanye called her and the conversation sounded kind of flirty and romantic. It could be that they are just good friends,' said the source.

But Pia, who was introduced to the rapper by Kim's youngest sister, Kylie Jenner, took to Twitter to explain their relationship: 'Kylie and her family are good friends of mine, I tried to ignore the media, but let me make it clear, the stories are completely false,' she wrote.

And Khloe Kardashian also chimed in, laughing off the reports that Kanye had been sneaking around with Pia: 'I know I'm late but seeing a rumor about Kanye & Kylie's teenage friend!' tweeted Khloe. 'They don't even work together! How do these rumors get started! LOL.'

The run-up to the wedding was proving to be a frantically busy time for the couple, who were thrilled to receive Anna Wintour's personal invitation to one of the biggest fashion events of the year – the Met Gala Ball in New York.

On the night the pair rubbed shoulders with some of the biggest stars of stage and screen at the ultra-glamorous event, but Kim stole many of the headlines in a revealing Lanvin dress slashed to the thigh.

When asked on camera by *Vogue*'s contributing editor André Leon Talley whether she had already married in secret, Kim explained: 'It's still Kim. Mrs West soon.' She also told him she had made her wedding dress choice. 'I tried on quite a few, [then I] narrowed it down,' she teased.

She also posted a photo of herself and Kanye alongside Anna Wintour, who co-hosted the event with Hollywood actors Sarah Jessica Parker and Bradley Cooper. Guests were charged $25,000 at ticket, $10,000 more than the previous year, and the theme was White Tie And Decorations, an ode to Anglo-American designer Charles James.

Guests were asked to pay tribute to the late couturier by donning high-end vintage looks, such as ball gowns and long gloves.

Kim took time out from the event to rave about Domenico Dolce – one half of fabled design team Dolce & Gabbana – writing: 'Domenico Dolce is one of my all time faves! We had so much fun discussing the gown he made for the *Vogue* shoot!

'His entire table was breathtaking and looked like the most perfect Dolce ad campaign! Monica Bellucci looked stunning!'

On a roll, Kim also referenced fashion designer Zac Posen after posting a shot of them together at the annual event, writing: 'Zac Posen took me to my 1st fashion event! Me, him & Pat McGrath.'

Donatella Versace also got a special mention from Kim, who posted a picture of the designer in an emerald green gown, with the caption: 'I love this woman! #donatellaversace' alongside a shot of herself with the iconic Italian designer.

Another fun snap showed Kim and an uncharacteristically cheerful-looking Kanye striking a pose with British model Rosie Huntington-Whiteley and Balmain creative director Olivier Rousteing with the accompanying message: 'Balmain babes'.

Then there were photos of her fiancé posing with Jay-Z, which she quickly followed up with another shot of the rapper and producer with Anna Wintour.

Next up was a model sandwich as Kim, who accidentally flashed her matching navy blue underwear as she made her way to the event earlier in the evening, stood in between Naomi Campbell, Cara Delevingne, actress Kate Bosworth and designer Riccardo Tisci.

She rounded up her Met Gala album with a shot of her posing with her little sister Kendall, who wore a stunning Topshop gown: 'Best thing in life is sharing memories with the ones you love! From getting ready together to experiencing the night I'm happy you were at my side @kendalljenner I love you my model baby!!!' wrote Kim.

All the stars were gossiping about the rumours that Kim and Kanye had already married in secret before the Ball, even British model Cara Delevingne was overheard, saying: 'Have they got married? I need to know. Is this their honeymoon?'

While Kim downplayed the rumours all evening, she was spotted deep in conversation with Balmain's creative director Olivier Rousteing, fuelling speculation that she might have chosen a cream sleeveless wedding gown from his exclusive collection.

Following her glitzy evening with Kanye, who wore a Charles James tuxedo with coat tails and changed the subject if anyone asked him about the wedding, Kim wrote on her blog: 'Last night was an amazing time at the Met Gala.

'I was in love with my Lanvin strapless dress. Alber Elbaz helped Kanye and I get ready for the evening, which was a perfect fit because he also dressed us for the cover of *Vogue*.

'It was such a tough decision on how to accessorize. I left the store with a chunky belt and leather cuffs. We were going back and forth for hours if the chunky belt was right. In the car on our way there we got a glimpse of the carpet, and I decided the accessories were a bit too "rock 'n' roll" and I wanted to go for something more simple and elegant.'

So, she concluded, 'I switched to a clean black satin belt and strappy heels at the last minute because to me it felt more classic and fit the Forties theme better. Kanye also liked it better too. Overall I thought it was the right decision and I loved the way everything came together.'

Her firm friendship with the chief designer at Lanvin led to speculation that Elbaz was also working on one of her three wedding gowns. Alber Elbaz is famous for his joyful yet feminine designs that seem to capture the essence of the moment in which they're worn.

The Israeli designer is also known to be a fan of *Keeping Up With The Kardashians*, telling *The Wall Street Journal* in 2012: 'At 10pm at night, all I want to do is come home and watch Kim Kardashian get a haircut.'

Unfortunately for Kim it also emerged that Victoria Beckham, one of her favourite designers, had turned down the opportunity to design a dress for the big day. Victoria claimed she was too busy, although according to *The Hollywood Gossip* website: 'Kim was desperate to wear a VB dress for her big day, but Victoria deals with the very A-list of the showbiz world, including royals, and doesn't want to be dragged into the world of reality stars'.

Meanwhile Kim went from one glitzy bash to another

that week – she then spent the evening at the USC Shoah Foundation's 20th anniversary Ambassadors for Humanity gala, where she met an Armenian genocide survivor, and said: 'Honored to be at the USC SHOAH Foundation event to support Armenian genocide testimonies. I'm sitting next to the most inspiring 100-year-old Armenian genocide survivor.'

But she had also been hoping to be introduced to President Obama, who received an award presented by director Steven Spielberg. But the US President – who has twice called Kanye a 'jackass', slammed the reality star's family, and turned down her offer to help out on his last presidential campaign – kept his distance at the gala dinner.

'Kim's table wasn't close to President Obama's,' a source reveals, but she 'enlisted one of her minions to scout out the opportunity to meet him.

'Obama's table and surrounding area was swarming with Secret Service, and security was very tight, and it was conveyed to Kim that she wouldn't be able to meet him.'

But after the President accepted the award, he stayed for dinner and Spielberg was allowed to bring several friends over to meet him. 'Kim was let down and disappointed,' the source revealed. 'She didn't understand why she couldn't just say hello to him [...] Kim truly thinks she is American royalty. She doesn't understand why President Obama wouldn't want to meet her.'

In 2009, the US President had called Kanye 'a jackass' for interrupting Taylor Swift's VMA acceptance speech, and three years later, he did the same again, during an interview with *The Atlantic* – 'He is a jackass. But he's talented,' the Commander-In-Chief said.

Obama also commented on the couple in 2013, saying, 'We weren't exposed to things we didn't have in the same way kids these days are. Kids weren't monitoring every day what Kim Kardashian was wearing, or where Kanye West was going on vacation, and thinking that somehow that was the mark of success.' Kanye fired back at the time: 'I don't care if you're the President, I'm from Chicago.'

But Kim and Kanye were not going to let a minor setback like that derail their wedding plans, as it emerged that the groom had put in a request to the French President, François Hollande, to use the country's official security forces who protect the highest national personalities and important foreign guests.

'He's asked for some of the 3,200-strong team to be dispatched to him for the day and has offered to pay $1 million for their services,' a source told *Heat* magazine.

Kanye reportedly wanted their guests to be subjected to a pat down and searched when they arrived at the wedding: 'There will be twice as many security staff than guests and metal detectors at all entry points. Kanye insists that everyone be checked.

'They will be monitored by CCTV and have phones and cameras confiscated.'

The star also wanted airspace over the French capital to be shut down to prevent paparazzi from getting exclusive shots of the big day.

The source told *Heat*: 'Kanye sees himself as the biggest star in the world and he wants to ensure that the city is prepared for "the wedding of the century".

'He wants to shut down Paris airspace on their big day and has even put in a request to the director general of the French Aviation Authority.

'His team are trying to warn him that it's unlikely to happen, but Kanye is convinced that their wedding is important enough. With the couple spending millions of dollars, he believes it should be granted to them.'

Kanye was also busy organising his own bachelor party, but could not seem to decide on an appropriate venue. A source told *The Sun* newspaper: 'Kanye loves Dublin, as does Jay-Z, and it's pretty close to Paris so it's a perfect option before the wedding.

'He has had his people looking into places like The Four Seasons and The Ritz-Carlton and clubs they could take over for a night.'

Kanye was thought to be keen to host a bachelor party in Ireland because he wanted some distance between himself and the Kardashian clan.

The source added: 'Kim will be doing her own thing with the girls and Kanye knows that in Dublin he would pretty much be left to himself.'

And it might have turned out to be a second bachelor party for the 'Bound 2' star as it had previously been claimed Jay-Z would be throwing him a lavish celebration at his New York club, 40/40.

Around the same time it was being suggested that Kim and Kanye were planning a civil ceremony at her mother Kris's

Calabasas mansion on their return from Europe. In fact, there were whispers that a secret formal wedding ceremony had already taken place ahead of their European celebrations. Despite their millions the couple had been prevented from legally marrying in Paris because neither was a French resident.

'Kim and Kanye are disappointed they can't officially marry in Paris,' a source told *Grazia*. 'But they will have an intimate ceremony with only their family at her mother's home instead. They want their guests to see them marry for the first time in Paris, which is why their civil ceremony is being kept hush-hush.'

Speculation mounted that the intimate private ceremony had taken place in California when pictures emerged of Kris at an LA branch of the supermarket Costco stocking up on enough toilet paper to sink the *Titanic*! Commentators suggested she was preparing to host a very important party at her home.

At the time the happy couple were staying at The Mercer Hotel in New York – and for once they did not seem to mind being photographed, prompting further speculation that they had recently tied the knot.

'The rumour was that Kim and Kanye had a very low-key official celebration at Kris's Calabasas mansion,' a Hollywood-based source told *Grazia*. 'There was talk that the no-frills ceremony was apparently attended by just a handful of close family and friends. Afterwards, guests enjoyed the couple's favourite foods: fried chicken, mashed potato and cornbread.'

Needless to say, Kim steered well clear of all the carbs on offer.

'Kim won't count herself as married until after the Paris

nuptials,' a source told *Grazia*. 'She and Kanye always knew they'd be legally required to get married in the US first, as they're not French citizens, but she saw it as a formality. She won't call herself Mrs West until they've had the big blow-out celebration, because she wants the world to see that as the main event.'

Despite their plea for privacy, details of the celebrations began to leak out in the run-up. It was even reported that they planned to erect a £200,000 mock Buckingham Palace balcony at the Château Louis XIV, where they intended to marry, in line with their Royal Wedding theme. And, proving money really was no object, there were also suggestions that guests would be sent home with goody bags containing £300 bottles of Bollinger champagne, £120 Crème de la Mer face cream and Swarovski crystals personalised with the bride and groom's initials.

Kanye was planning to arrive by helicopter, while Kim hoped to make her grand entrance in a traditional horse and carriage, it was claimed. Continuing with their theme, it was reported that they had hired carnival acts, as well as magicians to entertain their VIP guests, and Kanye had arranged a fireworks display. A vineyard had been tasked with producing a personalised champagne for them to toast with once they were married. They were inspired by Brad Pitt and Angelina Jolie who produced their own rose wine a year earlier. Called Chateau Miraval, it was made from grapes grown at their £35m estate in the South of France.

It came as no surprise that Kanye was said to be organising an equally lavish gift for his bride-to-be. The rapper, who is worth a cool £70m, was said to be buying a ten-bedroom eighteenth-century château that once belonged to the legendary French actress Catherine Deneuve. The £3.3m castle just outside Paris boasts a 700 square-foot master suite, sauna and cinema.

'Kanye knew his wedding gift had to be a show stopper,' the source also told *Grazia*. 'After looking at possible wedding venues around Paris, he decided that they should have a French home too. He fell in love with it and knows Kim will appreciate the Hollywood connection.'

Given the whole production was being staged on a dizzyingly grand scale, it was no surprise that the bride and groom were demanding complete discretion from their guests. One US report claimed that attendees had received a confidential 15-page document outlining the logistics of the day and stating: 'For our privacy, we are keeping the details to a minimum so there can be surprises for everyone.'

Another report claimed that guests would have their phones confiscated on arrival, and replaced with pre-paid handsets that can only dial pre-approved numbers.

And while it was unknown exactly where the couple planned to spend their honeymoon, insiders revealed that they were intending to take a lengthy break following the wedding: 'They're planning on taking some time off for sure,' a source told *People Magazine*. 'They're used to busy schedules but they want to have some downtime as newlyweds – and together as a family.'

But with Kanye scheduled to perform at the X Games in Austin, Texas, just two weeks after the wedding, the couple did not appear to have allowed much time for a honeymoon.

Other sources close to them suggested that they planned to stay in the City of Light, since it had long been their favourite place. Kanye has been a long-time client at Paris's most exclusive Résidence hotel, which boasts an A-list guest membership that has included Hollywood's Leonardo DiCaprio and Beyoncé. The pricey pad requires pre-acceptance just to access the hotel website, and rates run from 1,500 to 15,000 euros per night for the sky-view penthouse with a terrace.

The couple had also struck up close friendships with several Paris-based fashion designers, such as Givenchy's Riccardo Tisci, Stéphane Rolland, Karl Lagerfeld and Balmain's Olivier Rousteing. It was at Balmain where sources say they rang up more than $25,000 in pre-wedding accessories and gift purchases, back in April.

'They've visited many times,' one design-house source told *People*. 'Kanye will sit and talk about the art and styling for hours. He's knowledgeable, and Kim has been quietly visiting here for years, spending time in the atelier where the dresses are made. She's really interested in the process and is fascinated by the hand work and the details.'

And during their time together, the pair also narrowed down their favourite restaurants. They consistently chose the same two eateries – grabbing lunch at popular bistro L'Avenue, followed by fancy cheeseburgers at Ferdi's.

And shortly before the wedding party departed for Paris, Kanye was still hoping that his friend, and fellow rapper, Jay-Z would agree to be his best man. According to *Radar Online*, Beyoncé's husband sent Kanye a gold-plated, diamond encrusted hip flask that had an inscription referring to himself as 'The Best Man'. The flask was accompanied by a $10,000 bottle of Scotch for Kanye to sip on his wedding day.

However, Jay-Z had reportedly refused to attend the nuptials because he did not want his daughter Blue Ivy being filmed, leaving Kanye without a best man. But since the bride and groom decided that cameras would not be capturing the wedding, they still hoped to persuade him to fly to Paris.

'She's [Kim] taping everything else so she can get things for free in exchange for exposure,' stated a source to *inTouch* magazine. 'They realised how much their wedding was costing so they told *E!* they wouldn't allow parts of it to be taped unless the network offered them more than $15million, which is what Kim got for her wedding to Kris,' another insider reportedly told the magazine.

According to the same report, Kim had been 'cutting deals left and right' in order to minimise expenditure and maximise profits for herself and the rest of the family.

'Her mom couldn't help herself either. Kris is trying to get them another $4million for their wedding photos,' added the source, who also revealed that at Kim's Parisian themed bridal shower: 'The decadent food, drinks and goodies were paid for or sponsored by brands that wanted exposure. *E!* picked up the rest.

'Kim made millions off her last wedding on top of everything that was paid for,' the source explained. 'She understands the business of having a televised wedding.'

Indeed the ceremony with Humphries would have cost them $10million if they had to pay for it themselves. Instead the now-estranged couple earned millions from TV rights.

Despite the reports, Kim's mother Kris Jenner insisted her daughter 'didn't make a dime' out of the wedding. In an interview with *People* magazine addressing widespread criticism of Kim's previous nuptials, she said: 'The one thing that is the most annoying is the rumour that she made millions off of this wedding.

'She didn't make a dime and, actually, spent millions of dollars on the wedding – so it's not something that she thought would ever not be happily ever after.'

Kris went on to say that Kim would probably donate all of her wedding gifts to charity.

But this time around, 'momager' Kris was far less involved in the details of the day. In an interview just a week before the wedding, Kris admitted to *E! News*: 'Kim and Kanye have done this all on their own and they've had the best time planning it and I know nothing.

'I have not seen her wedding dress,' she added. 'I don't know how she looks in it. I'll see it for the first time when she puts it on at her wedding.'

Kris said she was excited to just be able to relax and 'let everyone else worry' about everything because she's 'such a control freak'.

'I'm going into this with a great deal of excitement,' she said. 'I was a little bit curious at first and now I'm just like OK, just let it go, breathe and enjoy.'

Scott Disick was also being kept in the dark to prevent any secrets leaking out. When asked if he had helped with the planning, he replied: 'No. I probably won't even have anything to do with my own if I ever have one.'

And when asked, the couple's friend Ryan Seacrest told *Access Hollywood*: 'Here's what I would guess. It would be one of the most amazing ceremonies that has ever been had.

'I think that we'll all sort of smile and love that fact that you can see how much he adores her and she adores him,' added the TV presenter, who had not received an invitation himself.

And there would be plenty of private moments too, as it was believed that Kim was planning on conceiving her second child on their honeymoon.

'She wants to get pregnant right after the wedding,' a source told *Us Weekly*. 'She wants her kids to be close in age.'

Many fans were surprised that Kris was not more involved in her daughter's wedding but in the past Kim has defended their feisty relationship, saying that although many people think they are harsh with their mother, they just try to be honest and try to keep things professional when they have to. Kim admits that she can be very direct when it's business related, and although their mother/daughter relationship can be a tricky one, she would not have it any other way.

CHAPTER 11

A CHANGE OF PLAN

Although they went to great lengths to keep plans under wraps, just weeks before the big day Kim and Kanye's wedding invitation was leaked to the press. It had gold lettering printed onto grey card, reading: 'The honour of your presence is requested at the marriage of Kim Kardashian to Kanye West'.

The initial invites had very few details, only the date and that the wedding would be a black tie affair, with a pre-wedding dinner and cocktails in Paris the evening before. All the rest of the details would be revealed to guests when they arrived in France.

But no sooner had the invitations been dispatched than rumours started to spread that the guests would be flown from Paris to Florence, Italy, by private jet.

Us Weekly warned readers that Florence might be just part of a grand wedding plan, not necessarily the final destination.

'Kim and Kanye have told all guests different info,' a source told the magazine. 'No one knows all of the details.'

But then a close friend of the couple let slip that the wedding was to take place at a sixteenth-century fortress with a tragic history, just outside the city of Florence. Kanye's pal, designer Ermanno Scervino, confirmed the venue, as the rapper revealed that he chose Florence because North was conceived there.

The hotly anticipated wedding was not due to take place in Paris as everyone had expected, but instead in the spectacular Forte Belvedere di San Giorgio Firenze, a fortress built for the ruling Medici family of Florence.

After two young people fell from the ramparts in 2006 and 2008, the authorities were prompted to close it to the public. It was finally reopened in 2013 and Kanye had been hard at work organising the surprise wedding, according to Italian friends.

Kanye knows the city well because he has clothes for his label made in the garment district and the couple holidayed there in 2012 to celebrate Kim's thirty-second birthday.

He told Florentine news website *La Nazione*: 'For me Florence is the most beautiful European city and one of the most beautiful cities in the world.

'But the real reason is that Kim and I were on the banks of the River Arno last year on our own, incognito. And I think that our daughter North was conceived here among the Renaissance masterpieces.

'It was as if it was our first honeymoon.'

Kanye added that he was feeling 'emotional' about the big

day. He went on: 'I'm quite emotional but also happy. I am a romantic.'

He had been staying with his Florentine friend Ermanno Scervino, outside Florence, while he made the final plans for the wedding, the designer's spokesman confirmed.

'It's true. Ermanno has been helping Kanye organise the wedding in Forte Belvedere,' he said. 'They met in Paris earlier this year and have become great friends.'

Shortly before the wedding Kanye spent several days in Florence, meeting with Scervino at the Italian designer's atelier, fuelling rumours that he would be wearing his designs to walk down the aisle.

Kim had not been seen in Italy but had been visiting Paris off and on for the past few months, apparently for wedding dress fittings at Lanvin.

Previously she had said that they were planning to tie the knot in Paris, but then it was revealed that the romantic French capital was only part of the plan. They relocated to the Italian fortress after being told that they were not considered distinguished enough for an official ceremony and celebration at the Palace of Versailles. Kim and Kanye had set their hearts on becoming man and wife in the world famous former home of France's pre-revolution kings and queens. But Catherine Pégard, président of the Palace of Versailles, said it just 'wasn't possible' – but allowing the couple a formal visit would be welcome publicity.

Ms Pégard said in a statement: 'Kim Kardashian and Kanye West have decided to visit the Château of Versailles with their guests in a private surprise tour organised for Friday, May 23rd, on the eve of their marriage.

'In making this choice, they will contribute once more to a better understanding of Versailles, and will help to maintain the exceptional heritage of Versailles, which is classed as a world heritage site by Unesco.'

So instead the couple had to make do with a pre-wedding dinner in Paris and a private chaperoned tour of the Palace of Versailles with their guests.

Vogue contributing editor André Leon Talley had also asked designer Valentino to host a brunch for Kim and Kanye at his elegant Château de Wideville in Paris on the eve of the wedding – and he would be covering the glamorous event for *Vogue.com*.

After dinner the guests would be whisked away in private planes to Florence for the actual wedding ceremony the next day, *Entertainment Tonight* reported.

In grey and gold wedding invitations that went out in April, guests were asked to wear cocktail attire for a dinner in Paris on 23 May at 6pm. But while the wedding location itself was still not officially disclosed, all eyes were on the Italian fortress, which was built in 1590 for the Grand Duke Ferdinando De'Medici to protect the city and to demonstrate the power and wealth of the family, but it also houses an elegantly designed villa.

Until the twentieth century it was used to garrison troops and then for exhibitions and events. The sweeping panorama over Florence from above the famous Boboli Gardens is among the city's most breathtaking. But in 2008 artist and filmmaker Veronica Locatelli fell to her death from the bastions in an unexplained tragedy. The 37-year-old had been celebrating her birthday at the bar, which was hosting a party to celebrate an exhibition by fashion photographer David LaChapelle. As she went to greet friends she was spotted by a security guard near the ramparts. The guard says that he called out to warn her to stay away from the low wall above the gorge, but his efforts proved futile for she slipped and plummeted 10 metres, suffering a fatal head trauma.

Just two years before, a twenty-year-old visitor from Rome, Luca Raso, who was holidaying with friends in the city, fell in the same location. He too died.

The centuries-old, star-shaped stronghold was immediately closed for an investigation and restoration works but after five years of renovation, the Belvedere reopened in 2013. Boasting sweeping views, it is often used as a venue for contemporary art exhibits. It costs around £300,000 to hire for a private event.

During the week leading up to the wedding, row upon row of boxes, crates and even a crane were seen outside the sixteenth-century fortress. Kanye was said to have laid on a luxury pool filled with pink water. And since the stronghold is located close to a sewage works, he had also ensured an air freshening system was installed.

An employee told *Radar*: 'They have gone to great lengths to make sure the place smells lovely.'

They had been given permission to invite a maximum of just 200 guests, Florence City Council spokesperson Elisa Di Lupo said. The couple had paid the city of Florence 300,000 euros, or $400,000, to reserve the fort for their special day and week-long preparations.

Di Lupo added that the funds would be used for cultural projects in the city.

Access to the fortress, which has stunning views of the Renaissance city, is nearly impossible, and the building can only be glimpsed from street level or from the adjacent Boboli Gardens. Authorities in Italy said no plans had been made for a civil contract required for a legally binding ceremony.

As work went underway at the fort, one source told *Us Weekly*: 'This is literally going to be Hollywood movie set level.'

'We are up to our necks with this wedding,' a worker from a local company added. 'The security surrounding this is huge. The organisers let us know day by day what they need.'

But the changing plans were said to be frustrating many of the guests, who were being kept very much in the dark.

'Everyone is confused,' an insider told *RadarOnline.com* of the couple's friends and family, who were all being told different stories about the extravagant soirée.

'Kanye is furious about the leaks. He wants to know who he can trust', the insider added.

Guests included close family friend Joyce Bonelli, who posed for photos in front of the Eiffel Tower with Kris, make-up artist and hair stylist Rob Scheppy, who was busy tweeting pictures of himself in Paris, alongside Kim's younger sister, Kendall Jenner.

TV presenter LaLa Anthony was also believed to be on the list and singer Ciara, a close friend of Kim's, would have been attending had she not given birth to a baby boy less than a week before the wedding.

A spokeswoman at the Florence mayor's office confirmed the new arrangements to the Associated Press just a week before the wedding. Elisa Di Lupo added that a Protestant minister would be presiding over the nuptials.

Despite Kim initially saying they wanted to keep their ceremony private, a source told *Radar*: 'There will be at least five cameras present at Kim and Kanye's wedding ceremony and reception, which will air on *Keeping Up With The Kardashians*.

'Yes, Kim did publicly say that they were keeping the wedding private, but momager, Kris Jenner, was able to persuade the couple to allow cameras to film,' the insider added. 'The couple will have the final say about how much of the event makes it onto the show.'

Kim had insisted that her wedding would not be televised, tweeting: 'We are not filming our wedding for *Keeping Up With The Kardashians*. You will see everything leading up til and after! Privacy is our main priority.'

As the couple touched down in Paris at the start of the week of the wedding, more details began to emerge about the day itself. It was reported that singer Lana Del Rey was being flown out for the pre-wedding bash in Paris, in return for a six-figure fee. According to the *Mirror*, Lana's hit, 'Young and Beautiful', is one of Kim's favourite songs. But the singer hit back at rumours she was paid up to $2.8million to perform three tracks at the lavish party: 'I would never let a friend pay me to sing at a wedding, that would be crazy,' she said. 'I'll do it for free, like I did this one.'

The couple asked the star to entertain their guests with

three songs after Kanye, thirty-six, hired an orchestra to perform her hit, 'Young and Beautiful', when he proposed in San Francisco on Kim's thirty-third birthday.

Four days before the wedding Kim arrived in Paris with daughter Nori and a jaw-dropping 12 huge suitcases, which were stacked up on a trolley and left to an Air France employee to struggle with as the reality star made her way through a wall of photographers.

She looked exhausted following an 11-hour overnight flight from LA, where she had walked straight into an animal rights protest, and was surrounded by activists holding up pictures of caged lab monkeys, whom they said were flown by Kim's airline of choice, Air France, to laboratories.

While Kim had previously been the target of a flour bomb attack by an animal rights activist, this time she was largely left alone as she headed to board her important flight.

Arriving in Paris she kept her daughter covered in a black shawl as she pushed her way out of the airport, before transferring the child into a waiting car. She left Charles de Gaulle airport, and went to meet up with Kanye for ice cream to kick off their 'wedding week'. The rest of Kim's family followed later the same day, with Kris Jenner immediately posting a selfie, riding a merry-go-round.

Kris had arrived with her own mother, Mary Jo, although Kim had not been sure that her grandmother would make it to Europe for the wedding, largely because she had previously admitted that she was not a fan of Kanye's: 'I was a little turned off at first because of what he did to Taylor Swift,' she said in an interview in 2012. 'But I have nothing to fault him with.'

But she and Kim are close and have a great deal in common. Like Kim, she has been married three times, first to her childhood sweetheart, and just like her granddaughter's wedding to Kris Humphries, it lasted a mere two months. However, her final marriage lasted 40 years before she was widowed in 2003.

Former model Mary Jo is also a savvy businesswoman, with a string of five children's clothing stores.

Mary Jo, who was on her first-ever visit to Paris, appeared to quickly get a grip on Parisian chic, impressing fashion commentators with a series of stylish monochrome outfits.

Of course the entire wedding party made sure they looked their best at all times. Designer Michael Costello had created several couture gowns for Kim's closest girlfriends, Brittny Gastineau, Larsa Pippen, Blac Chyna and Carla DiBello, as well as their outfits for the duo's big day.

The fashion designer told *UsMagazine.com* he was 'kind of shocked' when so many of the reality TV star's inner circle got in touch with him. He said: 'They were all competing [when they first came in]! They wanted to look their best. I think they just all want to show up and shut it down. They want to be there for Kim, but they want to look their absolute best.'

He added: 'We're not just making one dress, we're making two for each girl. They're all very romantic, really beautiful, structured silhouettes.'

Kim's little sister Kylie Jenner risked incurring Kris's wrath when she arrived in Paris with bright blue hair, telling *E! Online*: 'They're all really pissed. My mom was like, "You look like a Skittle".'

Also, on the Monday, 19 May, it emerged that the couple had managed to narrow their guest list down to family and close friends. 'The wedding is small and intimate. It's not going to be a big blowout like her last one,' a source revealed to *People* online. 'This wedding is really about Kim and Kanye and people who have known and loved them for a long time. And everyone who is invited just can't wait for the wedding week to begin!'

But according to other sources a stressed-out Kanye had offended some friends when he dramatically slashed the guest list at the last minute, as he started to realise just how much they were spending.

During their whistle-stop tour of Paris the couple were certainly not taking it easy. Trailed by an army of photographers, they spent $8,000 in a pre-wedding splurge on designer clothes. Four days ahead of the nuptials, a source told *E! News* they were: 'Gazing in shop windows and popping in and out of their favourite stores. Kim was smiling non-stop.'

After browsing the boutiques of Saint Laurent, Versace, Miu Miu and Balenciaga without making purchases, the pair bought a few items from Céline. A bystander said: 'Kanye was very supportive and would lend his fashion expertise while Kim was trying on clothes. She tried on a couple of asymmetrical skirts, grey sweatpants, and a gold square bracelet.'

Kim bought a $5,600 black skirt with pom-pom embellishments and navy and white striped skirt for $2,100, as well as a long army green skirt. She also took home a pair of new Mask sunglasses in orange for $420.

The pair then grabbed a bite to eat at upmarket restaurant

L'Avenue, as Kim showed off her pre-wedding body – which she had been honing and toning at the city's exclusive L'Usine gym – by going braless under a skimpy blush pink vest.

Later that day several Valentino bags were delivered to the couple at their hotel, but on the Wednesday Kylie and Kendall Jenner visited Saint Laurent, prompting fevered speculation about their bridesmaids' dresses.

Later the same day *E! News* reporter Ken Baker called into *On Air With Ryan Seacrest* to divulge a few last-minute details. He explained: 'What we know is this – everyone is there. Bruce [Jenner] will be giving her away.

'We don't know what dress she's wearing, she's been keeping that a very good secret.' As for the wedding party, Baker added: 'We do know her bridesmaids will be her sisters, the groomsmen will be Kanye's best friends from Chicago. I just talked to a guest and this person was extremely stressed out. They said to me, "I'm the kind of person where I need to know everything that's happening. They're like, be ready to leave town but just show up." And this person's like, "I don't know what to wear, I don't know what to bring." The guests are totally in the dark and that's what Kim and Kanye want.'

That day Kim also admitted she was worried that the stormy weather would ruin her wedding. A source told *UsMagazine. com* that the star was noticeably upset when she enjoyed dinner with her family at the Hôtel Costes before visiting the Eiffel Tower and a nearby carousel during a downpour: 'I hope the rain doesn't ruin my wedding,' she declared.

The onlooker added: 'She made it clear that this bad weather is really getting to her. She's clearly spending millions getting married in Europe, and if it all turns into a wash-out she will be really unhappy.'

Another insider said Kim had told family over dinner: 'This weather has to get better. Spring in Paris is meant to be about sunshine, but all we're getting is rain.'

But she still managed to have a fun hen night, treating her family to dinner at Hôtel Costes, one of the most expensive restaurants in Paris, where the crew reportedly racked up an eye-watering bill of more than 2,400 euros (that's $3,282.72).

At the lavish dinner, Kim appeared to have raided the iconic French queen Marie Antoinette's wardrobe for her bachelorette party in a bejewelled pearl-encrusted gown worthy of royalty. While the hemline may admittedly have appeared shockingly short to Marie Antoinette's eyes, the rest of the Balmain gown would not have looked out of place in her court.

After dinner they moved on to a private party at the Eiffel Tower – where else? Of course this was not a traditional hen party, there were no strippers or L-plates, but every moment was relayed by guests via social media. 'No matter what these girls are always there! #BFFS #OGCrew #ParisNights,' Kim wrote on one post, alongside pictures of her pals posing outside the Louvre and the Eiffel Tower.

They then moved on to Crazy Horse Paris, a famous burlesque club, with Khloe Kardashian, Kendall Jenner and Kim's girlfriends. The famed cabaret club is known for its raunchy stage shows performed by nude female dancers.

Khloe documented the girls' night out, Instagramming a sultry photo of herself and Kendall, whom she called her fellow 'masked crusader', as both girls were wearing black lace veils covering half their faces.

Kim also shared a photo of herself with her 'glam squad', thanking 'these talented gypsies [who] make me beautiful [and] make me smile from the inside out!'

Her publicist pal Simon Huck shared a sweet snap with Khloe, too, that showed him planting a kiss on the bridesmaid's cheek. 'No one better!' he captioned the pic.

The following day designer Rachel Roy, one of Kim's best friends, was pictured striding defiantly through LAX Airport en route for the wedding.

Just weeks earlier, Beyoncé's sister Solange Knowles brawled with Jay-Z in an elevator after the Met Gala, and it was reported that the fight was to do with Rachel's close friendship with the rapper.

With interest in the brawl (which was caught on CCTV and broadcast around the world) sky high, Beyoncé's dramas threatened to eclipse the wedding itself. In the end, Jay-Z and Beyoncé skipped the event, instead spending a quiet weekend in the Hamptons with his family. He and Beyoncé were seen arriving back in New York City two days after the wedding, and disembarking a helicopter with their two-year-old daughter, Blue Ivy. The couple sent an expensive bottle of Chianti with the cork replaced by a huge diamond stopper.

As Kim and Kanye's wedding got underway on the Saturday, Beyoncé shared a make-up free selfie from bed, while also showing off her long braids. But she did take time to wish the newlyweds well. She posted a photo to Instagram of Kim, Kanye and North, along with the words: 'Wishing you a lifetime of unconditional love. God bless your beautiful family.'

It was previously claimed by *Radar Online* that Beyoncé had declared that 'under no circumstances will she be a part of any filming on the wedding day' for reality television.

And that was not the only last-minute panic: 'They had problems with the bridesmaids' outfits because Kendall, Kylie and Khloe have all lost weight, while Kourtney has put some on, meaning the tailors had to work through the night,' a source told *Grazia*. 'Kim was furious.'

Kim's own pre-wedding wardrobe was no disappointment, however, as she showcased a series of high-end designer outfits in the run-up to her big day – no 'Bride To Be' emblazoned velour tracksuits for her!

Making at least three changes a day, Kim cherry-picked from the fashion industry's most exclusive designers. From her $20,000 Balmain dress to the high-maintenance suede strapless dress by Italian designer Ermanno Scervino, her wardrobe was expertly stage-managed.

When Friday dawned, all eyes were on designer Valentino Garavani's seventeenth-century château, on the outskirts of Paris, where *US Vogue*'s André Leon Talley was hosting the couple's pre-wedding brunch. Kim showcased a ravishing Maison Martin Margiela gown, but despite the joyous occasion Kanye looked furious as he was pictured leaving the Hotel George V en route for the castle.

Six hundred guests, including the Kardashian clan, family friends Jonathan Cheban and Simon Huck, music bigwigs like Rick Rubin and Guy Oseary, personal trainers Gunnar

Peterson and Harley Pasternak, as well as Lanvin designer Alber Elbaz (who dressed Kim for her *Vogue* cover and the Met Gala), arrived in a convoy of vehicles. Earlier guards had been seen measuring the distance that friends and family would need to walk over cobblestones.

After brunch, guests were treated a few hours later to a private tour of Versailles before packing their bags and flying out to Tuscany for the main event.

Following the last-minute change of venue, the wedding cake was smashed in transit: 'The cake was a huge, cream-filled white and gold confection but it toppled during the drive from Paris,' a source told *Grazia*. 'It's caused catering chaos.'

Some guests were heard to complain that the decision to move to Florence meant they had to fork out for return flights from Italy: 'Some guests were asking to skip the Florence leg and stay in Paris,' reported *Grazia*.

But of course it wouldn't be a celebrity wedding without a little hiccup or two. Kim's aunt, Karen Houghton, put her foot in it when she told *The Sun* that the wedding would have a Royal-inspired theme, reminiscent of the Duchess of Cambridge's style: 'Kim really loves Kate,' she said. 'Kim saw the visually stunning Royal Wedding and wants to replicate that. It's a great chance to show the world what a classy family we have.

'Kim might even wear a crown or tiara made from real diamonds. She'd look like an English princess. Kim and Kanye are a little bit like our Prince William and Kate.'

Perhaps it was no coincidence that Karen also revealed that she would no longer be attending the wedding.

CHAPTER 12

MR &
MRS WEST!

As the day itself finally dawned, security checkpoints were set up around Forte di Belvedere, in a bid to keep prying eyes away from the highly anticipated wedding. Once they passed through one checkpoint, guests were driven uphill across a cobblestone courtyard to a second gilded gate, where plumed horses and riders stood to attention.

As guests lined up to enter the wedding on Saturday, they all signed tough non-disclosure contracts and also handed in their mobile phones. Discussing the secrecy of the occasion afterwards, poet Malik Yusef, a friend of Kanye's who attended the wedding, said in *Grazia* magazine there were 'no TV cameras, no cell phones and we were scanned before entering.'

'That made it a cherished moment "out of the spotlight"', he added. 'The media has been venomous about the couple, but people there were full of love. You could say what you wanted to say, you could kiss who you wanted to kiss. These people worked like dogs to get here and now they have treated themselves.'

Hundreds of fans who had been waiting outside for hours broke away from behind barricades as the groom (wearing a beige suit with satin lapels) arrived at a side gate in a Porsche. Overexcited fans began surrounding cars and banging on car windows, shouting 'Johnny Depp!' and 'Beyoncé!'

Neither of those Hollywood stars were there, in fact celebrities were few and far between.

The Oscar-winning director of *12 Years A Slave* Steve McQueen, who wore a blue suit with a skinny tie, joined in the celebrations alongside fashion legend André Leon Talley, who sported a huge red cape. Actor Will Smith's son Jaden was there too, along with rapper Big Sean and LaLa Anthony, wife of New York Knicks basketball star, Carmelo Anthony.

US Vogue editor-in-chief Anna Wintour was among the high profile stars to decline an invitation to the lavish nuptials, but a spokesperson for Wintour insisted that it was nothing personal. 'Anna had a longstanding family commitment this weekend and sadly had to miss the wedding,' a source told the *New York Post*'s Page Six.

By 7.45pm, most of the guests had arrived, including the bride, and beyond the gates all that could be seen was a seven-minute fireworks show. But for the guests inside it was a lavish extravaganza: 'It was a roller coaster, but in the best way,' one guest revealed to *People* afterwards. 'It was a crazy, nonstop, incredible dream.'

But there was at least one quiet moment during the ceremony, when the couple recited their self-penned vows, which featured 'a little bit of humour and a whole lot of love,' added the attendee.

'The groom told me he had practised them in front of a mirror several times to commit them to memory,' revealed the source. 'He didn't make any mistakes.'

And the couple's 11-month-old daughter, North, made sure to capture the spotlight as she was carried down the aisle by her grandma, Kris Jenner: 'She clapped the whole way down,' a source said later.

While they celebrated their nuptials in grand style, they sealed the deal with the sweetest simple gesture: a kiss. In a photo revealed by the couple, they locked lips amidst a wall of flowers as their pastor, Rich Wilkerson Jr., looked on.

In another, the Givenchy-clad duo were holding hands while walking down the aisle as a married couple to the cheers of their guests.

The ceremony, which included opera singer Andrea Bocelli serenading as Kim walked the aisle, was 'beautiful' and 'so romantic,' long-time family friend Malika Haqq told *People*.

And with the eyes of the world on the wedding of the year, Kim made sure she was picture perfect by hiring old friend and celebrity make-up artist, Mario Dedivanovic.

Fresh off the plane from Florence, he explained how he achieved Kim's flawless look: 'I did her make-up for her wedding and it was amazing,' he said.

Mario, who met Kim on a make-up shoot in New York over five years earlier, said that despite the global audience he had not been nervous about the very important role he had played in her wedding.

'We worked together for so long so I'm so comfortable with her face. It was actually not nerve-wracking. It was a great experience. She looked stunning,' he added.

Despite a gagging order preventing him from revealing any secrets about his friend's third trip down the aisle, he did reveal how wonderful the celebrations had been: 'It was a magical weekend. I can't really speak of any details. To put it in one word, it was magical. It was amazing. I am very happy for her.'

To get chiselled cheeks and a flawless face like Kim on her wedding day, however, Mario divulged his secrets: 'Contouring frames the face and chisels the cheeks. So basically it's putting a little bit of bronzer on the hairline and jawline and on the hollows of the cheeks and the bridge of the nose. It thins out the face and gives warmth to the face,' he explained.

'Sometimes it takes 20 minutes, sometimes an hour. The most important is to blend, blend, blend,' added Mario.

'Usually we look at what she's going to be wearing or the event she will be attending. I take inspiration from her outfit and her hair,' he revealed.

As well as having Mario on call throughout the week, Kim spent hundreds of thousands of dollars flying her entire entourage out to Europe for the wedding. Make-up artist Rob Scheppy explained: 'There are three or four of us that now work consistently with Kim and the entire family,' he said. 'Their family is so big, so you can't do everybody every day. We go into a rotation based on scheduling.'

Hair stylist Michael Silva, best known as the brains behind actress Jennifer Aniston's famous 'Rachel' haircut, styled Kim's hair for the MTV Movie Awards in 2013 and he was enlisted to create her wedding hair on the big day and for her hen party in Paris. Kim and Khloe often use stylist Jen Atkin, who also works with Jessica Alba, Emma Stone, Jennifer Lopez and Katy Perry, but she was also getting married the same weekend as Kim – in Paris.

Another hairdresser, Scotty Cunha, was also flown over as part of the glam squad and documented every detail of the trip on Instagram and Twitter with highlights including tweets: 'ALL HAIL THE QUEEN' and 'I am literally so happy with how naturally gorgeous I look in all these paparazzi shots #parih'.

Fashion stylist Monica Rose was there too, having described Kim as her 'muse' in 2010 to *Grazia* magazine: 'Her personal style was completely different before I began working with her,' said Monica. 'But she is so open-minded and willing to take fashion risks. It's rewarding to see the evolution of her style and see she has grown into her own sense of style.'

One of Kim's best friends, make-up artist Joyce Bonelli, did attend the wedding, but she embarrassed the reality star just a few days earlier when she flashed her breasts at Kim's bachelorette party outside the historic Louvre Museum.

Joyce has been working with Kim since before *Keeping Up With The Kardashians* ever aired, and says fame hasn't changed the star: 'Some people get crazy, but Kim is the exact same person she was then: so sweet and caring and polite.'

Make-up artist Rob Scheppy was there to work with

Kendall and Kylie, having first met Kim when he was asked to do guests' make-up at a Victoria's Secret fashion show. He told *Grazia* magazine: 'There were a bunch of celebrities on the list that I knew, like Kim Kardashian, Kourtney Kardashian, Paris Hilton and Kristin Cavallari,' he said afterwards.

Never one to do things by halves, Kim was said to have had a spray tan using diamond dust. St. Tropez had launched the world's most expensive spray tan, which combines diamond dust with traditional aerosol tanning dye, several months earlier. The tan contains real diamonds, giving skin an iridescent glow.

The brand's tanning expert, Jules Heptonstall, revealed all the details about the one-of-a-kind treatment: 'The Diamond Tan is without a doubt the most luxurious tan possible – when performed I quite literally am spraying my clients with diamond dust!' he said. 'We now reserve the treatment for VIPs only. VIP brides for their wedding often request it.

'After the St. Tropez classic spray tan has developed and the skin is gorgeous and golden, I use St. Tropez Diamond Dust and lightly spray and buff onto the shoulders, the arms, the chest and the back to give an all-over luminosity and glisten – it's pure luxe.'

The bride and groom both wore outfits by Givenchy's head designer, Riccardo Tisci, for their Italian nuptials. Kim, who made her entrance 25 minutes late, wore a stunning mermaid-silhouette gown featuring delicate white lace. It was custom-made by Givenchy Haute Couture. Small panels of a sheer lace decorated the arm and also accentuated her slimmed-down waist.

The backless dress was long-sleeved with a train, while a dramatic flowing white cathedral-length silk veil completed the look. North's custom-made Haute Couture creation was made to resemble her mother's dress, while Kanye wore a bespoke black tailored evening suit.

The couple gazed at one another as their vows were said under the direction of Rich Wilkerson Jr., an associate pastor at Trinity Church in North Miami. Rich has been friends with Kim and Kanye since the couple attended one of his services, two years earlier – and he also happens to be best friends with *E! News* correspondent Jason Kennedy. Rich later tweeted that he was 'Grateful for their friendship. The best is yet to come.'

Faith has always been important to Kim, who as a child attended Bel Air Presbyterian Church. After Robert Kardashian died and the family moved home, Kris actually set up her own church in an old movie theatre at the Calabasas Commons shopping centre, with the help of her former minister, Pastor Brad. 'It's a wonderful church, not all high and mighty, just come as you are. That's where we go to church now, and Pastor Brad even married Khloe and Lamar,' said Kim.

During the ceremony famed Italian tenor Andrea Bocelli serenaded Kim and Kanye with several of his songs, including the neoclassical 'Con Te Partirò' ['With you I will leave'].

Kim's bridesmaids, her sisters Kourtney, Khloe, Kendall and Kylie, were all dressed in white, although their dresses did not match. They sat front row next to mother-of-the-bride Kris Jenner, also in white, and Bruce Jenner, who like most of the male guests wore a black suit.

Grandmother Kris held baby North on her lap, while Kourtney had little Penelope on hers.

And in the first wedding pictures Kim's adorable daughter is seen watching as her parents walk down the aisle after getting married.

After saying their vows, and exchanging Lorraine Schwartz wedding rings, they took a moment to replace the fancy tuxedos and lace with edgy black 'Just Married' leather jackets. The newlyweds made use of their wedding photo booth to share snaps of the fun biker jackets – said to have been ordered by Kanye as a wedding gift. An endearing black-and-white photo showed the pair standing with their backs to the camera. Kanye – whose jacket read 'Just' – glanced over his shoulder, while Kim – whose jacket read 'Married' – stood by his side.

According to *E!*, who released the image, artist Wes Lang, who created a bird-like silhouette containing a strike of lightning beneath the text, customised their matching jackets.

Schott NYC was the designer responsible for the jacket worn by Kanye, while Kim's similar one was made by BLK DNM.

A series of other jaw-dropping photos from the wedding of the year were also released by *E!*, giving the first official glimpse into the couple's extravagant occasion.

One heart-warming image showed Kim and Kanye kissing after exchanging their vows, on the backdrop of an enormous 20-foot high wall of white roses – a bigger version of Kanye's Mother's Day gift to Kim. *People* reported that the floral arrangements came from a store in Florence, Fiori della Signoria, and cost more than $100,000.

The newlyweds also shared a snap of a romantic kiss in the photo booth.

Speaking moments after the ceremony *to E! News*, Kris Jenner said she was: 'Beyond bursting with happiness for Kim, Kanye and baby North.

'Such a magical, romantic wedding!' added Kris. 'I feel blessed to have my new son and his family as part of ours.'

And Kanye seemed equally excited, with a source telling *MailOnline* that he gave a 45-minute speech to the gathered guests. Introducing his bride, he announced: 'I just wanna stop the music a second 'cos my baby's coming back with a new dress on. Here she is – Kim Kardashian West.'

Following the ceremony, Kim changed into an embellished Balmain gown.

As he continued with his lengthy toast, Kanye described Kim as: 'The ideal celebrity, the ideal art.' He also told his guests they were, 'The most remarkable people of our time.

'They feel like it's okay to put you on the tabloid covers to sell your image, to use you in an SNL spoof. We don't negotiate. We're not like that. We're not stupid. The Kardashians are an industry,' he said.

'We are warriors! There is not one person at this table that has not had to defend us at some point or another. At this table the combination of powers can make the world a better place.'

After the ceremony, the guests broke bread together, sitting family-style on a 70-metre-long marble banquet table – a gift from master craftsman Gualtiero Vannelli, who used marble from the Tuscan quarry in Carrara, according to *Us Weekly*.

And as Kim finally relaxed her strict low-carb diet, they feasted on traditional Italian food with an 'innovative' twist. The menu included homemade mezzaluna pasta stuffed with ricotta, herb-crusted monkfish filet, beef fillet with Brunello di Montalcino sauce and potato tart seasoned with truffles, followed by strawberry sorbet.

Guests sipped on both rosé and gold Armand de Brignac champagne, as well as Brunello di Montalcino San Filippo Le Lucere red wine, which sells for over £50 a bottle.

The food was colour-coordinated, with pink being the theme. And the meal culminated with a towering seven-foot high wedding cake of white sponge and white icing with fruit layers, reported *People.com*.

Celebrity photographer Nick Knight, who has a long history with the couple as he was the director of the infamous 'Bound 2' music video, posted an Instagram from the wedding with the caption: 'It was a pleasure to be a part of it.' But he was there as a guest, not as the official photographer. That honour went to Conor McDonnell, who was whisked to Florence after being sworn to secrecy and made to sign a confidentiality clause not revealing any details of the stars' wedding although he did allow the happy couple to later reveal a selection of his pictures via their own Twitter and Instagram accounts.

McDonnell's wedding pictures quickly became the most 'liked' in the history of Instagram with more than two million people giving them the thumbs up on Kim's account, beating the previous record holders, Justin Bieber and Selena Gomez. Their photo, posted in January on Justin's Instagram of the now-former couple and captioned, 'Love the way you look at me', received 1.82 million likes.

Kim and Kanye's wedding kiss was retweeted almost 100,000 times on Kanye's Twitter account, and a staggering 114,000 people favourited one of the wedding pictures.

McDonnell began his career by shooting local bands while he was still at school in Liverpool, before becoming Rita Ora's official photographer and the British singer-songwriter introduced him to Jay-Z and U2.

'Rita is awesome,' Conor said. 'I've been doing loads of work for her – videos, photos, promo work. She's a really great person to work with and be around; very fun, cheerful, down-to-earth, it's a good laugh.

'The first time I photographed Rita was when she supported Drake at the Echo Arena. I'd heard some of her stuff before so was pretty excited to see her as I'd heard good things about her live.

'A few weeks later she was back in Liverpool on the DJ Fresh tour. I got asked to come along and do a video for her. I got to hang out with her backstage and we took some portraits, did a few bits for the video and got on really well.'

Conor has subsequently gone on to become Ellie Goulding and McBusted's official photographer, as well as doing work for Biffy Clyro, The Stone Roses and Robbie Williams.

Although on the day the couple appeared to have been delighted with the photographs, Kanye later revealed that it took four days to perfect the pictures that were released to the public, after celebrity photographer Annie Leibovitz pulled out the day before.

Speaking at the Cannes Lions Festival, he said that Leibovitz had changed her mind about taking the wedding pictures just a day before the event, meaning fans had to wait days for the first official photograph, called 'The Kiss', to be released after undergoing extensive retouching. During a panel discussion about technology and culture, he said he still wanted the pictures to look as much like hers as possible, as he remains a huge fan.

'I'll tell you a little story about the Kiss photo that my girl put up,' Kanye told a packed audience of hundreds. 'We – and this was p***ing my girl off during the honeymoon.

'She was exhausted because we worked on the photo so much because Annie Leibovitz pulled out of the wedding, because I think she was scared of the idea of celebrity.

'But because Annie pulled out, I was like, "I still want my wedding photos to look like Annie Leibovitz's photos", and we sat there and worked on that photo for four days – because the flowers were off-colour and stuff like that.

'Can you imagine telling someone who wants to just Instagram a photo, who's the number one person on Instagram, "We need to work on the colour of the flower wall", or the idea that it's a Givenchy dress, and it's not about the name Givenchy, it's about the talent that is Riccardo Tisci – and how important Kim is to the internet.

'And the fact the number one most-liked photo [on Instagram] has a kind of aesthetic was a win for what the mission is, which is raising the palette.

'It was a long time,' he added – drawing laughs from the audience.

'The Kiss' photo eventually received more than 1.93 million likes, and more than 35,000 comments.

Other famous guests on the day itself included *Girls Gone Wild!* founder Joe Francis and his girlfriend Abbey Wilson, and John Legend tweeted a photo booth snap of himself and wife Chrissy Teigen with the caption 'Love, love, love'. The singer-songwriter serenaded Kim and Kanye with his song 'All Of Me' for their first dance.

Kim later posed with Balmain designer Olivier Rousteing, and John Legend took over festivities as the party began in earnest.

The singer said in a speech: 'To Kim and Kanye. It's really inspired me to be here. All these wonderful people here – it's a celebration of your love. I've seen Kanye with other women. I'm serious, this is a bad speech, but I have never seen him as into someone as he is into you, Kim.

'He was so into you before he was even with you. He is in love with you. I am so happy to see you two together.'

From inside the party Giancarlo Giammetti, honorary president of the Valentino Fashion House, shared snaps of the happy couple as they took to the stage to greet guests.

Guests admitted they were surprised that there was no sign of Kim's brother, Rob Kardashian, who had shocked everyone when he flew back to LA from Paris on the day of the wedding, skipping the proceedings entirely. The twenty-seven-year-old wiped clean his Twitter feed after fleeing the weekend's extravaganza.

Conflicting reports suggested that Rob's weight were the reason he did not stick around for the wedding. On an episode of *Keeping Up With The Kardashians*, Rob admitted he gained 40 pounds after his break up from singer Rita Ora.

An insider told *HollywoodLife.com*: 'Rob is not in a good place right now at all and his family should be very worried about him. He was embarrassed to go to the wedding in the first place because of his weight gain.'

Friends said his confidence had been severely knocked since he started piling on the pounds, which was the result of his 2013 break-up with singer Rita Ora.

He was said to have felt so insecure at having not been able to shed any weight in the lead-up to the wedding that he shunned the event just to avoid being in the family photos.

However, two days after the wedding Rob was back on Twitter, not to congratulate his sister but instead to send his well wishes to his one-time best friend and partner in crime.

'Happy Birthday @ScottDisick! Love You Brother!' he captioned a photo from a 2011 family trip to Bora Bora of himself riding a trike through water, with Scott sitting in a tub on the back.

Indeed, Rob seemed to be seeking solace in the closest thing he has to brothers.

'Rob really misses Lamar, he was like a big brother to him,' a source told *MailOnline*, adding: 'Lamar really helped Rob with his problems when it came to wanting to lose weight, and they've never lost touch.'

Despite his absence from the big day, Kim has in the past spoken fondly of her only brother, saying: 'No matter how old Rob gets, he'll always be our baby brother. Ever since he was born, all of us girls wanted to baby him. We're all so maternal.

It was only natural – he was the only boy in the family and he was the youngest, three years younger than the youngest of us. He really was the baby!

'Our dad's name was Robert so people called Rob "Baby Robert". In fact, they called him that until he was fifteen. Poor guy.

'Rob will always be much younger than we are, and boys are "younger" than girls in general, as in less mature. And since he's been around all these girls who pamper him his whole life, he's used to being our baby. Let's face it, he loves it.

'Although he didn't like it when we were kids, we used to dress him up like a girl. We tortured and teased him so much.'

Although Lamar was not at the wedding either, he rang Kanye to congratulate him shortly after the ceremony. According to *HollywoodLife.com* the former basketball star was one of the first people to call to give him a few words of encouragement: 'He called Kanye about four times and on the fourth call he actually got through.

'All Lam said to him was, "Hey, man, congratulations. Take care of Kim and the family, they're all good people."'

Kanye apparently responded by saying simply: 'Thank you' before getting off the phone to re-join his new bride. The source told how Lamar was still coming to terms with the fact that he's no longer in a relationship with Khloe, and missed her supportive family: 'It's no secret that Lamar misses Khloe and being around the family. He thinks they're good people and they have embraced Kanye just like they did him when he was married to Khloe.

'They're a family and they put each other first. Lamar misses that connection he had with them because he didn't grow up like that.'

Gradually over the days following the wedding more details began to emerge despite the couple's plea for privacy.

Vogue's contributing editor, André Leon Talley, told *Watch What Happens Live* about the moment when the couple kissed at the altar: 'It was extremely long, which is always a good sign. I would say there was probably tongue engagement.

'I think this relationship has a lot of legs. I'm looking forward to the next baby, which will probably be called South or South West,' he joked.

Another detailed report told how the couple chose a grassy ridge at the top of the Forte di Belvedere for their ceremony. Because they did not want to be married at an accessible part of the fort they hired a crane to lift every single item used in the wedding up 70 metres (230 feet) to the very top.

The biggest decorative element of the wedding was a giant gold box, 15 metres (49 feet) tall, which contained the bathrooms. It was situated right next to the dinner tables at the reception with a bar in front of it. According to one Italian source: 'Their toilet was the star of the show.' The Italians named it the *Torre di Bagni Oro*, which translates as the Gold Toilet Tower.

It was also revealed that instead of place cards, they had a team of Italian stonemasons engrave the name of each guest into the marble of the long dining table, in front of the individual place settings. The mammoth task was only finished late the night before, and, unfortunately, the wedding planners misspelled a few names.

Four days before the wedding Kanye ordered 30 life-size nudes to be made from black marble from Carrera. The marble workers worked through the night to cut enough blocks, but ten of them fell apart, another ten were too damaged in transit to put out, and of the remaining ten, four were missing their heads, but they were nevertheless displayed around the dinner tables.

Kanye made a visit to the venue two hours before the wedding, while the statues were being set up and insisted the marble nudes be moved a little further away from the dinner tables. Since each piece weighed half a ton, the whole crew spent the final two hours struggling to get them moved to precisely where he wanted them. Since time was tight the forklifts were the first thing guests saw on arrival.

And although the festivities appeared to go off without a hitch, behind the scenes there had been a series of last-minute tantrums and narrowly avoided disasters.

When Kim checked out the venue a few hours before the wedding a spotlight beamed onto her crotch area, and she was so angry that she apparently ran over to the electrical boards and unplugged the entire circuit. This shut down half the lights on the cocktail area. It also turned out the lights in the bathrooms, so the Gold Toilet Tower was dark inside, and everyone was too afraid to plug the lights back in.

Kanye also decided at the last minute that he did not want the 80 moving lights that he had ordered to illuminate the dance floor, declaring, 'I'm in the centre of this party, and I'm the only one people need to see. The rest of these people don't need lights on them.' The lights, which had taken four days to install, were all removed, and a crane was needed to take them back down the hill.

Just one hour before the wedding the groom decided that he did not like the all-white bar, and according to eyewitnesses he actually started sawing it in half himself. Two Italian construction workers were ordered to hold the bar stable as he sawed at the front, shouting that it looked like a bar from Texas. He then ordered two pieces of raw wood to be nailed onto the front of the bar. Once the wood was in place he said: 'Now it's art.'

During the same visit Kanye also inspected the £100,000 sound system, and decided he did not like the look of the speakers and wanted them hidden: 'You Italians don't understand my minimalist style,' he told them. As a result the entire system was pulled out as the first guests were arriving, and the wedding music had to come from an ordinary iPod until after dinner.

However, when John Legend played his set, he sat at a custom-built marble piano as the couple danced alone to five songs, including his hit, 'Ordinary People'.

According to a report in the *New York Post* Jaden Smith wore a white Batman-style cape and smashed several glasses, while *Vogue Italia*'s editor in chief, Franca Sozzani, was becoming increasingly irritated because he kept coming up behind her and throwing his cape over her head.

But Kris Jenner leapt to Jaden's defence, telling *HuffPost Live*: 'He is the greatest kid in the world. I'm very close to Jaden and he's like one of my own, you know.

'He had this Batman costume on and I thought it was just

genius,' she added. 'When you look at it, it sounds just crazy, but it was beautiful. He looked so good, and so fun, and he also has a really good sense of humour. It added humour to the night.

'It was almost like, "Oh, there's Jaden in his Batman costume". It wasn't like a crazy thing.'

'He saved my life the next day,' she added. 'Because I lost my suit and shoes I had gone to Florence in – I couldn't find my clothes. I happened to have a pair of jeans and a jacket and shirt to leave in. But I had no shoes, except my Giuseppe Zanotti shoes that Giuseppe gave us to wear walking down the aisle, but I couldn't wear those home.

'Jaden came walking out of the hotel and I said, "Jaden, where's your Batman boots?" And I borrowed them!

'So, Batman saved the day.'

There were also reports that one guest, a woman in her fifties, was so drunk between the ceremony and dinner that she collapsed and an ambulance was called. Another guest was seriously hurt after falling over at the top of the Belvedere tower. She had climbed in the hope of catching a glimpse of Justin Bieber although he was not actually invited to the wedding.

Later in the evening Kanye presented Kim with a special wedding gift – a raunchy portrait of herself wearing nothing but skimpy underwear – specially commissioned from London based artist Bambi to mark the occasion.

'It's the first non-narcissistic thing Kanye has done because he specifically didn't want to be in the painting himself,' a source told the *Daily Star*. 'Kanye has said he doesn't care how much the painting costs. This is likely to be Bambi's biggest sale to date.'

Bambi's manager Leonard Villa explained how Kanye's brief was short and sweet – apparently he told the artist to make something 'regal but typically Kim'.

'This has been done on metal and just completed in time for the couple's return,' he added. 'It was a recent commission and Bambi has turned it around in three weeks. The request came through an agent and the fee is in five figures. So far it's a one-off but we weren't told the image had to remain exclusive, so she could have more in the pipeline.'

Some days after the event the cost of the whole weekend was estimated at a staggering £6m, including £238,526 to hire the Forte di Belvedere, £44,127 per aircraft to fly guests from Paris to Florence and back and £177,778 for Kim's Givenchy wedding gown.

Her dress for the pre-wedding brunch at Valentino's château was worth around £49,000, while the Balmain dress Kim wore for her hen party cost £7,155. The couple also spent £1,100 per room per night for the 200 guests and £2,450 for Kim's hen dinner at Hôtel Costes. The seven-tier wedding cake was thought to cost £2,385.

CHAPTER 13

THE HONEYMOON

After the wedding Kim and Kanye surprised their fans by shunning super-yachts and the hottest nightclubs, and heading instead to rural Ireland for a relatively low-key five-day long honeymoon.

After their private jet touched down in Cork the day after their wedding, officials confirmed that they had checked into the Castle Oliver estate in Ardpatrick, County Limerick, where for weeks preparations had been underway for their arrival. Kanye had requested that the hotel install a mini office and a recording studio so that he could carry on recording, should inspiration strike during the holiday.

He also demanded a new fitness suite and extra security cameras around the perimeter of the property. And according to sources in Ireland he splashed out £3,000 on a personal trainer so that he and Kim could enjoy private workout sessions. Their private jet was waiting on stand-by in a nearby airfield so they could leave any time they wanted.

According to *Grazia*: 'Kanye treated Kim with a surprise gift on each of the first three mornings.' The presents included a £35,000 Cartier watch and a pair of Dior diamond earrings.

While the rest of the Kardashian family were making the most of the last of their wedding break by going sightseeing in Paris, the newlyweds were determined to have an authentic Irish experience. They were even spotted sipping on pints of Guinness in what could only be described as a fairly ordinary holiday. Although they both took a personal assistant and a bodyguard each, their entourage kept a low profile as Mr and Mrs West visited pubs, the cinema, went mountain biking and had picnics.

The couple were spotted looking happier than ever: 'What surprised us the most was how normal they appeared – Kim had ditched the high heels and skin-tight dresses for jeans, flats and no make-up (but still looked gorgeous) while Kanye appeared to live in his black jeans,' said a reporter for *Brides Magazine*. 'And cue the cute factor: nearly every time we caught sight of them they were hand-in-hand as they wandered around the hotel.'

The pair, who have visited the area before, did not join the other guests for pre-dinner cocktails in the eighteenth-century hotel's library, although they did head down to the dining room for lunch several times. For dinner, they mostly ate in the gorgeous Gold Room (Kanye's favourite, apparently), enjoying a menu that included Carlingford Lough Lobster Bisque, Irish Black Dexter Fillet of Beef and Valrhona Chocolate Delice, all prepared by Bronx-born chef Ryan Murphy.

The five-star hotel nestled in the Cork woodlands is steeped in history and set within 220 acres of beautiful land. Staff said they 'could not comment' on whether it was Kanye who had booked the Presidential suite – featuring a spacious bedroom and a lavish bathroom that boasts a large walk-in shower, full bath and its own sauna. On its website, the hotel states that the suite could cost the newlyweds upward of £40,000: 'This single magnificent suite has stunning views of the twelfth-century castle and ornate gardens to the back of the hotel.

'It features all the lovely touches of luxury found in the Staterooms and Grand Suites.

'The Presidential suite is ideal for entertaining with a separate sitting room, an anteroom generous enough to host a cocktail reception and a dining room all serviced by a dedicated elevator so that meals may be delivered directly from the kitchen below.'

The hotel also boasts 10-room treatment spas, a fitness studio, a Ron Kirby-designed golf course, four restaurants, and 800-year-old castle ruins. It has 103 bedrooms and suites, many of which have sweeping views of the parkland and lakes.

The hotel website adds: 'The eighteenth-century classic manor house lies adjacent to the ruins of an 800-year-old castle originally built by The Knights Templar under Richard Earl de Clare, known as Strongbow.

'The Resort is nestled in 220 acres of mature landscape, with meandering streams, parklands and a tranquil lake that is abundant with wildlife and gardens that include a reconstruction of the historical, classical parterre beds.'

Although they visited for less than a week, Irish tourism

chiefs were quick to cash in on one of the world's most famous couples honeymooning in the country. Marketing director Mark Henry said: 'We're working hard to produce a guide for their fans about where they are, or rather where they might be.

'We'd love to be able to give their millions of followers the information so maybe they can follow in their footsteps. It's a global story.'

When news first emerged of the superstars arrival, Mr Henry posted on his Twitter account: 'A big welcome to Ireland @KimKardashian and @kanyewest from all of us at @ TourismIreland – we're working to improve the weather right now...'

Tourism Ireland is hoping to run a potentially massive and lucrative marketing blitz by using a guide to places to visit to connect with just a fraction of the couple's millions of followers.

On their first day, Kim and Kanye went trekking and mountain biking before going to a local pub for a pint of Guinness. The newlyweds and four of their staff arrived at a popular mountain biking company in Ballyhoura, County Limerick at 8am. They then hired bikes for 35 euros each, along with a 75-euro tour guide, before trekking through the famous Blackrock Loop and the Ballyhoura Way.

During the day they stopped to enjoy a Taste of Ballyhoura hamper specially prepared for them by staff at The Old Bakehouse in Bruff. The treats from seven local producers included Ballyhoura Trekker's Tart made with smoked ham, Irish Cheddar cheese and served with a spiced apple chutney, as well as gluten-free sausages and black pudding – made from locally farmed pork. The hamper also included hot dishes such as Mountain Bikers' Mussels and Nature Loop Soup. A Honey and Hazelnut Nougat Cheesecake served with fruit compôte is thought to have been included in the lunch, as well as a lighter lemon posset. Instead of local beer they sipped on Ballyhoura apple juice.

They then made their way to a local pub, where the newlyweds enjoyed a pint of Guinness. Manager of the outdoor activity group, Fergal Somers later confirmed that they left a four-figure tip.

Mr Somers said: 'We had two American VIPs here yesterday. They had four staff with them. They only booked the day before. They went hiking and biking, as this area is well known for it. One of the party had visited the region before so knew about us that way.

'The guide said they had an absolute blast. He took them to the pub afterwards, where they had a pint of Guinness, I believe. They were very generous with their tip – I was told it was four-figure. There were six of them in the group, though.

'I don't know where they were going afterwards. They stayed in Castle Oliver before coming here, though.'

After spending their first night at the Castlemartyr Resort in Cork, the happy couple spent two nights at Castle Oliver in Limerick, where Siobhan Byrne Learat, of travel agent Adams & Butler, arranged their luxurious stay: 'It was a great honour to arrange a beautiful visit to a few of Ireland's most gorgeous locations and grand residences for them,' she said afterwards. 'I cannot comment on any of the details except to say that yes,

Adams & Butler were asked by top US agents we work with to put together a wonderful trip for them.'

They concluded their visit with one night in Laois, at the luxurious Ballyfin Castle. The pair then flew out of Cork Airport by private jet to Prague in the Czech Republic for another wedding. Before they left, Kanye presented his new wife with a traditional silver Claddagh ring as a memento of their stay in the Emerald Isle. Claddagh rings are cast in the shape of hands clasping a heart and crown, which symbolise friendship, love and loyalty respectively. This symbol of true love was identical to the one Bruce Jenner brought for Kris on their honeymoon twenty three years earlier.

Cork store executive Marie O'Connell told how she spotted their plane waiting on the runway, and noted their cortège as it swept in: 'I couldn't believe it. I saw them arriving in the limo and I managed to video it on my camera phone. I'm a huge fan, I'm still shaking, I'm so excited,' she said. The couple were whisked to the aircraft in a black Mercedes minivan escorted by a security car. They boarded the plane out of sight of the assembled media but, in the minutes before they left, Kanye sent one of his personal assistants into the airport duty free to purchase a number of Irish-themed gifts for family and friends.

Before the end of the honeymoon Kim took the time to change her Twitter account name to Kim Kardashian West. An insider told *E! News*: 'It was just a totally different part of the world that they had never experienced. They were engrossed in the environment and they enjoyed being able to escape.'

The pair were later spotted arriving in Prague for the

wedding of Kanye's stylist Renelou Padora, with Kim almost stealing the bride's thunder when both ladies were seen wearing metallic gowns on the same evening. Earlier that day Kim and Kanye toured the city, with Kanye showing off his simple gold wedding band for the first time. Kim, meanwhile, was not wearing her own band as it was being resized, but her hard-to-miss 15-carat engagement sparkler was still in place. Just eight days after they had tied the knot, Kim was seen without her new husband as she arrived back in New York City before connecting to a flight home to LA to be reunited with her daughter, who had been cared for by Kris.

Kanye made his way to Austin, Texas, where he was headlining the X Games, four days later. Insiders claimed Kim was less than thrilled by her honeymoon in rainy Ireland and had been hoping for a more glamorous holiday to match her fabulous Italian wedding and chic pre-wedding festivities in France. Kim had reportedly fallen in love with Ireland in 2012, when Kanye was there on tour and she flew over to surprise him.

'How the couple ended up in gloomy Portlaoise is a mystery to me,' revealed a source. 'It consists of flat midlands, working-class villages and very little to write home about in the way of touristy sights.

'Not only did they skip the touristy stuff, they also spent an entire afternoon riding mountain bikes on the muddy and treacherous trails in the Ballyhoura Mountains, north of Cork. And that couldn't have been very romantic, not with two assistants and two bodyguards in tow!'

The source claimed that by day four Kim was so bored

with her ho-hum honeymoon that she asked Kanye to fly to Prague a day early: 'Kim's idea of fun is getting dressed up and going to some great restaurants, and shopping till she drops in some of Europe's most posh boutiques. Not roughing it in the country. Once they landed in Prague, and Kim had a chance to get decked out in her finest again, she seemed a lot more content.'

And as soon as the couple were back home, it emerged that they were trying for another baby because Kanye wanted a son.

His stepbrother Hal 'Gore' Carmichael spilled the beans about the rapper's family dreams, and having a little boy growing up to be just like him was part of those dreams. This is something that Kanye's legions of fans will not be surprised to hear. In fact, part of the pre-nuptial agreement between him and his new wife, Kim Kardashian, was allegedly about children. Sources claim she was considering North being an only child, but he was insisting on one more.

The problem for Kim was that her pregnancy with North had been extremely difficult. She had gained weight, she was in pain and she just did not enjoy it. Although Kim has said she always wanted a large family, having grown up around sisters, Carmichael suggested to *Life & Style* magazine that he would keep asking his wife to produce more children until they had a little boy to keep his name alive.

Amid rumours that Kim had not been impressed with rainy Ireland, two weeks later he whisked his new bride off to Mexico on what was branded their 'official honeymoon'.

In June it was revealed that the pair had jetted south to

continue their post-wedding celebrations in Punta Mita, at a private beachfront residence in the village. An insider told *People Magazine*: 'They're staying in a private house on the beach.'

The spot is a favourite of the Kardashian family, and the fact that they flew out for another holiday just weeks after their last break was certainly interesting.

But Kim insisted she enjoyed her Irish break after arriving back in LAX without her husband. She tweeted: 'Had the best, most relaxing romantic honeymoon in Ireland & Prague! Missed my baby girl so much! Excited to be home to squeeze her so tight!'

When a fan asked why they had chosen Ireland for their honeymoon, Kim explained: 'We spent Kanye's bday in Ireland and fell in love with it! It's such a calming relaxing place!'

Although they must have hoped for a little privacy on their unexpected trip to Mexico, it was widely suggested that the couple were trying for another baby while enjoying their romantic holiday.

A source told *Us Weekly*: 'I think Kim will definitely have another baby soon – she wants to.'

In an interview with Ryan Seacrest Kim admitted that she wanted more kids but said she couldn't 'do more than three tops'.

The vacation was also to celebrate Kanye's thirty-seventh birthday during the trip, and before they left Kim took to her Instagram account to wish him a special day: 'Happy Birthday to my husband and best friend in the entire world!' she wrote. 'You have changed my life in more ways than you know. The way you look at life inspires me! I love you so much!!!!'

On the day itself Kim hung out backstage while Kanye performed at the Summer X Games in Austin, then surprised him with a custom-made *Yeezus* cake, and his very own man-cave, which she had had built in their new home. She also treated herself to what was being termed a 'booty room' dedicated to the upkeep of her famous derrière!

Kim wanted to ensure that she had a space of her own, and with so much of the house being dictated by Kanye's specific tastes, a personalised gym seemed the logical choice.

Speaking to *Grazia* magazine, a source said, 'The room will have butt-toning gym equipment, including the ProForm Booty Firm, the Yukon Fitness Butt and Thigh Shaper, the Suzanne Somers ButtMaster and a range of butt-toning belts and resistance bands.' And on top of all the high-tech gadgets there would also reportedly be a 'dedicated cellulite-busting area' with a laser machine, and a 'bum spa', which would be a pampering and treatment area for her bottom, for when the workout got too tough.

She even hired a 'butt expert' in addition to her personal trainer, to be responsible for her exercise regime every day. For years Kim's personal dermatologist had been giving her 'bottom facials', including exfoliations, steam extractions, oil massages, masks and moisturisers, but following her wedding the reality star felt it was time to step up the maintenance on her most famous body part. In the past there had been reports that she had had implants and fat injections, and had hired a special butt tailor to alter skinny jeans for her curves.

There was also talk of a new 'glam room' for Kim too, which was allegedly costing $750,000 and would play host to Kim's 24/7 squad of hair stylists and make-up artists.

And it emerged at the same time that Kim and Kanye were endeavouring to be perfect parents, and had drawn up a lengthy list of rules for nannies charged with looking after their precious daughter North West to abide by. The protective couple want to ensure that she is given the best upbringing so they even hired a tutor to give the twenty-three-month-old French lessons.

'If Kim's family aren't home when the tutor arrives, Kanye would get furious,' an insider told *Heat*. 'They want Nori to learn French, as they'll be spending a lot of time over there.'

Kim and Kanye, who insiders have described as 'perfectionists', are said to be encouraging their baby girl to speak by using flashcards with words written on them, which they like to be held in front of Nori.

Also on the list, the magazine claimed, is regular exercise for their daughter, which the couple monitor when they are away, using an iPhone app: 'It's not like she's running around like a sprinter, but she has to be kept active – crawling and playing with toys from an approved list that stimulate her mind and body.'

The fashion-conscious pair also have a pre-approved selection of clothing for Nori to wear on a day-to-day basis so that she can look just as stylish as her parents.

'Her clothes are co-ordinated with shoes, and no carer is allowed to deviate from a pre-approved outfit,' the source added.

And unsurprisingly when Nori turned one in June 2014, the family pulled out all the stops to celebrate her first birthday. Indeed her parents sparked controversy by having her ears pierced and lavishing her with expensive diamond stud earrings.

The shiny gemstones were revealed for the first time when Kim and Kanye took their daughter to The Children's Museum of Manhattan, where five floors of literature, science, media and art exhibits awaited.

While piercing children's ears is a controversial choice, in some cultures it is seen as a traditional step for young girls, although it is not usually a typical practice in Kim's Armenian heritage.

Kim matched her daughter by wearing big diamond stud earrings, and she made a point of wearing a gold 'North' necklace in honour of the special day, which happened to coincide with Kanye's first Father's Day. Afterwards, she gushed about their celebrations on Instagram.

Along with a cute picture of Kanye and Nori cuddled up, sleeping side by side in matching grey outfits at the end of their busy day, Kim wrote: 'This is what life is about! Our baby girl turned 1 today! We played so hard they passed out while we were watching the game! Happy Father's Day to the best daddy in the world!

'The way you love our daughter and protect her makes me filled with so much love! #BestDayEver #Twins #HappyFathersDay #HappyBirthday.'

Grandma Kris Jenner also posted a sweet shout-out to mark baby North's milestone. 'You are an angel and I love you so very much!' she wrote on Instagram. '#lovebug #pinchthose cheeks'.

But just two days later a former nanny, whom Kim had shared with Beyoncé, told *Life & Style* magazine that: 'She [Kim] brags that Nori is cuter than Blue Ivy,' she claimed. 'She loves it.'

The ex-employee went on to say that Kim has strict rules when it comes to North's appearance, especially when she is out in public: 'Kim dresses her daughter in only neutral colours.

'Kim demands her posse walk behind her.'

But as always the family time together in New York was short-lived because the next day Kanye was on another plane heading back to France for an appearance at the Cannes Lions Festival. During an interview he revealed that he had to be with wife Kim Kardashian because she is the 'number one woman in the world'.

He said: 'I can't be with any girl but Kim because that's the girl I look at her pictures the most, I get turned on the most.'

Kanye's touching admission came in a conversation with Steve Stoute, Stephanie Ruhle and Ben Horowitz at a talk entitled 'Translation: Technology, Culture, and Consumer Adoption: Learning to Read the Cultural Landscape' held at the Palais des Festivals during the biggest advertising festival in the world.

In the same interview Kanye went on to explain that the public did not fully understand their relationship until they appeared on the cover of *Vogue*: 'You have to be able to take the lashes when people don't understand.

'Two years of people not understanding an interracial relationship, two years of people not understanding the idea of the art world meets the pop world, you have to take the lash and be able to swim in the backlash.

'I get bashed so much but create so much, just know that if you want to be a boxer you're going to get your face beaten constantly but then you may end up being a Mayweather or an Ali at the end of the day.'

Going on to discuss his controversial video for 'Bound 2', which featured his wife sitting topless on his lap while he rides a motorbike, he added: 'I still take a bashing for the "Bound" video. I always say that if *Vogue* had come out before the "Bound" video then everyone would have been like, "Oh, it's okay", and that's the endorsement.

'It took something established like *Vogue* to make everything okay and we had to wait. Like we had the wedding and then they were like, "that's cool now" because they were told by people who endorsed it.'

Kanye went on to explain: 'Throughout my entire life because of the way my parents raised me, I was like, "I have to work with the number one". I can't work with anyone but Jay-Z because that's the number one. I can't represent any company but Louis Vuitton because that's the number one.'

He continued: 'Before Obama, there was Jesse Jackson, there were different people talking about blacks, particularly in America that were not allowed to drink from the cleanest fountain, to work with the best resources. It's like Michelangelo told he's not allowed to carve with marble but told he's got to use cement or something like that.'

He was also asked his views on celebrity culture, explaining: 'I hate the one-off, [...] I am a lot of things but I am a celebrity and we are treated as rentable, like a one-off, just enough to advertise a product and get it out.'

Classic Kanye, and it left the world wondering what he would come out with next. But as this couple, who appear to be the very definition of what it means to be a modern celebrity, share their every move with their fans, we will know soon enough.